EVERYONE PRETEND TO BE NORMAL

NAVIGATING THE WORLD OF AUTISM

ROCHELLE MILLER

Connor Court Publishing

Ballan, Australia

Connor Court Publishing Pty Ltd.
PO Box 1
Ballan VIC 3342
sales@connorcourt.com
www.connorcourt.com

ISBN: 9781922168269 (pbk.)

Front cover: "A Normal Day In The Miller Household" by Annah Stevens

Printed in Australia

CONTENTS

This book is dedicated to my gorgeous guys:
Small, Medium and Large

Foreword (1)

Amid irreverence and humour is the touching account of a young family's story of living with Autism Spectrum Disorder. While this book will provide an interesting read to some, others who have taken this journey will be struck by the eerie similarity with their own experiences. Despite the diversity of ASD and the impact it has on individuals and their families, Rochelle's story is similar to thousands of other families who have also experienced ASD. Despite this, so many families feel alone, isolated and shunned by the community and professionals. Further, in a country which prides itself on its wealth and resources, families continue to navigate a system full of incompetence and inadequacies. I hope parents will read this book and feel empowered and supported. I hope the community will read this book and appreciate the difficulties experienced by these families and offer assistance rather than indignation and indifference.

Dr Robyn Young, Associate Professor,
School of Psychology, Flinders University,
Adelaide, SA

Foreword (2)

I have been working with people with ASD and their families since second year University way back in 1986. In that time, I have learned the most from parents who have a child on the autism spectrum and people who themselves have a diagnosis. Their passion, tenacity and positivity in the face of adversity is something that I have always admired and respected. Rochelle Miller's account of her journey with Caleb and Noah, along with the support of her husband, is one of those stories that inspires. Personal accounts like this often provide hope and comfort to other families travelling a similar journey. It should also serve as a text book for the many professionals that still have limited understanding about ASD and the impact that it has on people's lives. Rochelle's account of her ongoing battle with medical professionals, educators and the like is not an uncommon story. Many people find themselves in similar situations and the support from extended family and the broader community is not always readily available or accessible. This needs to change. There are many families who have not written a book but their stories are just as important, just as interesting, just as challenging, just as distressing, just as enlightening. Giving voice to these stories improves awareness and understanding. Rochelle's book provides a vehicle to tell one such story that represents the experience of many. I hope it paves the way for a better future for people with ASD and their families.

Jon Martin, Chief Executive Officer,
The Autism Association of South Australia Inc.

Preface

As a Clinical Psychologist, I have seen and experienced first hand the wonderful array of gifts that the Autism Spectrum provides and the myriad of challenges that also inevitably follow. I am in a fortunate position to be a part of many families' lives, often from the point of diagnosis, and then periodically through the different developmental stages of a child's life. I have witnessed incredible successes and achievements by the children that I have seen, and I have also felt and heard the ongoing frustrations relating to the current support system in this country, which is often viewed as poor and disconnected.

I am immensely pleased that Rochelle has provided us with an autographical account of her family's story and the complexities involved in raising her two wonderful children on the Autism Spectrum. I hope this story provides a level of insight and understanding for those in the beginning stages of diagnosis and a level of comfort for those who are in the midst of the often whirlwind that occurs in day-to-day life. I also hope that this book provides a level of connectedness for families and an opportunity to become aware that they are not alone.

The Spectrum is long and vast, and with it comes a large variety of differing needs. Some needs are clear to see. A child once walked into my therapy room, screaming at the top of his voice "I'M NOT ANGRY", as he began systematically grabbing and chucking every item that he could lay his hands on. I often see children on the Spectrum who have poor emotion regulation skills, in terms of their ability to identify feelings and to release them appropriately.

Some needs are not so clear. I remember a young girl who when at school would completely and emotionally shut down in a near totalistic manner. The child refrained from eating, drinking or going to the toilet during her day at school. In actual fact, the child's anxiety was so intense, she was literally internally combusting emotionally and she held on to her emotions until she could finally release ferociously on those who were safest in her world – her parents at home. Her mother told me that this uncoiling usually began in the car on the way home. Interestingly, in a corresponding school meeting, quite a number of eyebrows were raised when I suggested there might be a problem at school for this girl. I was told that from all visual reports at school, she appeared to be functioning exceptionally well – quiet and obedient and that perhaps her parents might benefit from attending a parenting course because the child's negative behaviours "clearly" only occurred at home. Can you imagine the frustration for these particular parents?

The acceptance and understanding of a child's needs with an Autism Spectrum Disorder can be immensely difficult at times. One mother told me the story of her attending a large family gathering with her child who had recently been diagnosed with an ASD. When they arrived, the Grandmother said to the young boy with delight, "I've made your favourite dinner especially for you – lasagna!" The boy became visually excited and immediately sat at the dinner table with increasing anticipation. The Grandmother went to great lengths in terms of decorating the large dinner table, complete with a beautiful clean white table cloth. As the large group of family members sat down at the table, the young boy took his first big mouthful of his Grandmother's lasagna and then promptly spat out all of the contents to different parts of the room, hitting a variety of people and objects. "THIS IS NOT THE SAME AS MUM'S!" – the boy yelled. The meltdown then followed, as did the looks around the room with eyebrows raised. The mother correspondingly heard a family member comment quietly to another that "all the child needed was a good smack." The mother and her child left early and she commented to me that she had never felt so alone at that point.

As children with an Autism Spectrum Disorder grow, so to do their needs change. Individuals with ASD can have strong cognitive abilities and an often unwavering intense focus on fixations and obsessions. During high school there often appears to be a disconnection with the school system. Keeping teenagers at school can be difficult because they often don't see the point in attending because it is perceived as flawed and inadequate. One of my clients with a fixation on Japan and its language bluntly asked a Japanese teacher how long she had taught the subject of Japanese. After the teacher's response, he then stated his surprise that after all those years of teaching she still couldn't teach the language right! The child struggled with the perceived incompetence and it wasn't long before he spent more time in the principal's office than in the classroom.

I remember clearly an individual who was struggling at school to the point of almost failing. I often use a boat metaphor for those who are struggling whilst at school, as a boat can be likened to their perception of school. It can be rocky, sometimes outdated, old, and uncomfortable. This reflects how individuals can often be out of step with the school system and the myriad of social cues that are involved with large numbers of children being in the one general space every day. Sometimes, the schooling system just doesn't seem to fit right and they often have no desire to learn about perceived irrelevant subjects.

Using the above metaphor, the frequent rocky seas often make an individual to want out/off. The issue is that many of the individuals that I see are quite intellectual and sometimes gifted and need an opportunity to practise/work in their area of obsession or interest. Without this opportunity, individuals can feel lost and mental health symptoms, such as depression and anxiety, can occur. We need to support individuals diagnosed on the Autism Spectrum to find a way through, to help them stay in the boat and to get them to the other side – whatever that other side may be (a Tafe course, university, employment or the like). I believe this to be crucial. I remember one individual who was struggling with high school and was about to drop out. With a proper structured management plan he managed to reach the other side. I bumped into him again some years later at a local university. He was now at the top of his class in his field, winning many awards. He was a man of little words – but his sentence to me that day and connected smile were enough: "Thank goodness I stayed in the boat". This illustrates that with the right intervention, wonderful things can happen.

My clinical practice involves ongoing learning and education. Whilst a portion of growth is related to the numerous courses and conferences I attend, a primary learning source is from the people who I believe know intimately more than the professionals in this field – the parents who are at the coal face. The contents of this book will highlight this point repeatedly throughout Rochelle's, Ben's, Caleb's and Noah's journey. Rochelle's kind willingness to express intimate details about her family's experiences will ultimately help others during the whirlwind of life and their own journeys.

Jason Leffers,
Registered Clinical Psychologist,
B.Psych. (Hons), M.Psych. (Clin)

Introduction

After years of reading about and researching the subject of Autism Spectrum Disorder (ASD), I find myself wanting to know how other families' daily lives play out, while parenting children with such a varied and pervasive disorder. My husband Ben and I have two boys Caleb (nine) and Noah (eight), both with ASD. Caleb was diagnosed when he was five with Asperger Syndrome and Noah at age two with autism. Initially I read factual texts outlining diagnostic criteria and behavioural strategies, then I moved on to any biographical and autobiographical accounts I could find, while always keeping a close eye on media attention focused on autism. Yet, I still find I have a desire to share domestic experiences with other families living with this rollercoaster disorder. We are fortunate to be closely involved with other families who also have children "on the spectrum", but it has taken some years to cultivate these close friendships. Initially we felt we were out in the social wilderness, and still do sometimes!

1

So I wanted to write a book celebrating the uniqueness and quirkiness of each and every family living with autism. Of course, I can only draw on our experiences of this, and feel I am better equipped to do this now with some sense of humour, than when dealing with that first initial diagnostic shock several years ago. In doing this, it is by no means my intention to diminish the pain, relentless exhaustion and at times despair, felt by parents of children with autism. Nor do I wish to offend anyone with a disability by using terms such as "Aspies" to describe a person who has Asperger Syndrome. This is a term that we use endearingly to describe our sons, and I understand that many people with Asperger Syndrome have adopted this term to enhance their identity as an emerging sub-culture. I am also aware that many people with Asperger Syndrome don't identify with their condition being a disability, but rather an exceptional set of *abilities*, in a more positive outlook. That is of course the right of the individual to determine, however it is also our right as parents of children with autism to recognise this can presently be a disability for them, as it is now widely recognised. If they choose one day to disagree with us on this point then we will respect their decisions and would welcome this self-awareness. I have also heard the term "Autie" used to describe a person with autism, and for us this can handily rhyme with *naughty* if necessary.

Whilst on the subject of phraseology, it is now considered to be correct to refer to a person as *having* Autism Spectrum Disorder, and not as that person as being *autistic*. They are people foremost who happen to have a disorder; likewise a person can have a disability and not be a disabled person, and so on. It can become a terminological minefield, and I only usually refer to my own children or my very close friend's children as sometimes being autistic, when it is clear that I don't mean this disparagingly; it is just an easier term to use at times. Incidentally, the whole language and diagnostic process of ASD is undergoing a major shake-up with the expected release of the new DSM 5 (The American Psychiatric Association's Diagnostic and Statistical Manual for Mental Disorders).This is further fuelling divisiveness and controversy among the autism community, with the possibility of merging Asperger syndrome into the blanket diagnosis of Autism Spectrum Disorder.

As I am by no means writing a textbook, I am simply aiming to inject some much needed levity into a very serious subject. I also want to emphasise that each child on the spectrum has incredibly varied skill sets and challenges, and that no doubt our experiences will not be common to everyone. I have read some amazingly inspirational and heart wrenching stories about triumphing over the hurdles of autism, and I am sorry to say that this story probably won't be one of those! Our children are not profoundly autistic and are considered "high functioning", if you favour that term, which I don't particularly. Such a simplistic label cannot adequately describe a person's strengths and challenges when talking about the complexities associated with autism. Therefore we don't have those odds to overcome; we just have the endless daily grind of trying to fit our "diamond pegs into round holes". More about that later.

So rather than being an educational or motivational book, although if it is that would be a welcome bonus, I hope my book illustrates that there is no right or wrong way to parent children with autism, there is just *YOUR* own way.

Our story is no more unique or sensational than many other families that I know of; I think every family living with disability has a book waiting to be written. I just needed to write ours now. At the risk of sounding a bit whacky (well a bit *more* whacky anyway),

I had a dream one night about writing this book, and then woke up the following morning with the book's title, synopsis and chapter plans burning a hole in my brain. So I began writing it the very next day. Maybe it was my subconscious processing all those times when people have suggested to me that I should write a book about our experiences – so I have. I sometimes also get told "I don't know how you manage Rochelle. I couldn't do what you do!" And I get embarrassed by this, because I know many people with much tougher situations than ours, and I know that we all just do what's put in front of us. Those that think they couldn't *would* manage too, and surprise themselves in the process.

Finally, I also need to say that I think for many parents with children with disabilities, it can be difficult to get our message across without invoking misunderstandings from those with differing viewpoints. While Ben and I do not always love the behaviours our children engage in, and we strive to improve and optimise their skills and quality of life, we do not wish that they were different children. Autism has made our boys the unique individuals they are, they can attribute some of their best qualities to their autism, and we are well beyond the stage of wishing that they were born with "Neurotypical" (NT) development. I can appreciate that many parents have not reached this level of acceptance, and some may never, due to their circumstances, hardship and enduring challenges. I simply feel fortunate that despite the obstacles, I now feel somewhat at peace with our lot, but still reserve the right to indulge in a good old whine (and a wine) at times. And this may just be one of those times!

1

Caleb's Miraculous Conception, Pregnancy Problems with Both Boys and Noah's Dramatic Birth

B en and I were ready to start a family after three years of living together and a further four years of marital bliss. As I am five years older than Ben my biological clock was in hyper-drive, so we were disheartened when our first conception took over a year to eventuate. Sadly this resulted in an ectopic pregnancy when I lost both the baby and one fallopian tube. I was under the care of a leading obstetrician when I began to have some concerning bleeding, so I attended a production style appointment for an internal ultra-sound investigation.

I was directed to a cubicle to disrobe (yes completely!) and then instructed to inadequately preserve my modesty with a flimsy, slashed-down-the backside robe. Then to my absolute amazement it was back out to another public waiting room, full of similarly attired and extremely embarrassed pregnant women who were desperately trying to keep their knees firmly locked together, while clutching at the back of their robes. I waited my turn for a very perfunctory internal ultrasound, and let's just say that involved a large uncomfortable plastic, rather phallic shaped device. I was then coolly advised by the obstetrician that he could not find the baby in my uterus where it should have been safely cocooned, so just to go home and to await the inevitable miscarriage. I did proceed to miscarriage, very painfully and dangerously. I did not want to attend that same clinic so I presented at a different hospital where I underwent immediate emergency surgery, as I was losing a substantial amount of blood with the ectopic pregnancy.

My initiation into the sometimes bizarre hospital world began upon my morphine induced awakening from surgery to a room full of young interns. The leading doctor, who had a serious God complex, thought it would be amusing to engage his underlings in a Jeopardy style game of twenty questions, with the unusual explosion of my unfortunate tube being the topic. I thought I was still in a drug induced coma, and then began to *wish* I was. I will say that I have come across a myriad of health professionals, from the most amazingly compassionate and proactive ones to the most mind-blowingly insensitive.

After my recovery we did seek some legal advice regarding what we felt was the obstetrician's negligence, and the lawyer agreed that we had a strong case. However, during her investigations she was baffled by the hospital's claim to have misplaced my initial internal ultrasound results. She advised us that we could still proceed, but it would be a long, difficult case to prove. We dropped it as we felt this wouldn't assist in mending our broken hearts and knew that we were not alone in having suffered this type of loss.

Miraculously Caleb was conceived a short time later, and it was full steam ahead into parenthood. Being the meticulous type that I am, I felt quite smug that I would quickly master this motherhood business, and really didn't know what all the fuss was about. Generational mistakes in our families were not going to be repeated by this alpha mum. Famous last words. Neither Ben nor I have ASD, but continuously get asked where our children inherited their autism from. One less than tactful person once suggested that we had " hit the jackpot", and I can only surmise that she meant that in a sympathetic way, as we certainly haven't hit any financial jackpots resulting from autism. Another more complimentary theory is that we both must be really intelligent, as only people with above average IQs (Intelligence Quotients) have children with autism, and we have two so we must be super brains. I prefer to hang onto this theory, yet to be scientifically proven but I am hopeful that there is merit in it.

I don't want to enter into the whole raging debate about whether autism is caused by genetic or environmental factors, or various combinations of both. I know some parents are adamant that their child's autism was induced by administering childhood vaccinations, and others claim it was present from birth, but I honestly don't know the cause. I have read very convincing arguments for many causal reasons, and can only attest to our own experiences. Let's just say that in our family there are a few autistic skeletons in the closet. The gene pool was perhaps a little bit murky on the days that we conceived our sons, and I have never attributed our boys' autism to the vaccination process. Nor do I believe that a person can be "cured" of autism, but developmental advancements can certainly optimise the prognosis for some people with ASD.

Caleb was a typically stubborn "Aspie" even before he emerged into the world. During the latter stages of pregnancy with him, I discovered he was in a breech position and was advised to undergo a procedure called an external cephalic version (ECV) to try to turn him around in utero, in preparation for a natural delivery. The obstetrician (a different one this time) confidently informed me that most babies will turn after this procedure, and that he hadn't come across too many that retained their initial position. So we dutifully trotted along to the hospital at our appointed time and I was then injected with medication designed to relax my uterus; in my newly relaxed state I wasn't worried when the kindly elderly doctor informed me that I may feel a "little bit of discomfort" during the procedure. He then proceeded (with the aid of his evil accomplice midwife) to pummel, twist and attempt to stretch my already painfully swollen abdomen.

I was having serious doubts as to whether my pain threshold was up to any of this pregnancy business, and just when I thought I might begin to scream with the agony, it was over. The now not-so-kindly doctor washed his hands and said in a matter of fact way: "Well *that* baby doesn't want to move so you'll be having a caesarean my dear." A caesarean! I thought. "No, no, no that isn't in my birth plan! Super mums don't have *caesareans*." They emerge triumphantly after hours of gruelling labour, glowing with joy and serenely nursing their newborns. *That* was what I was going to do. Instead I started to gently weep and was brusquely reprimanded by the doctor: "It's no big deal, you'll be fine" and off he swept in a swish of his white coat. How could I explain, even to Ben, that I felt I had failed at the first hurdle of motherhood: if I couldn't even get the method of birth right, what hope was there? Caleb just didn't want to relinquish his lovely, cosy warm position and he had no intention, even then, of succumbing to any external demands made on his time or comfort.

Not much has changed. To this day he still has a love of warm, dark cubby holes, and can often be found curled up under a table or in a corner with a blanket over his head and his army of soft toy "bed friends" piled on top of him. I had learnt my very first, extremely valuable and painful, lesson in relinquishing any level of control over my children. I was to fight this process for some time yet, and continue to do so in many ways. Now at least I have learnt to pick the battles I may win, and apply that perfectionist streak to more constructive tasks. By the way, the birth was fine, quite peaceful in fact, and Caleb was born a slightly jaundiced and petite six pounds eight ounces with the most beautiful huge blue eyes imaginable. We couldn't fail to notice, however, that his neck was twisted at a right angle and he could not move his head. We were quickly reassured that this was a temporary condition called congenital muscular torticollis, and was result of his having retained the same position in the womb for a long time! He was stubborn and requiring sameness even then. We rectified his neck problem after a few months of daily physiotherapy exercises, and he now has a lovely straight head that can swivel in a 360 degree motion, à la *The Exorcist!*

Many parents recall their children with autism as being remarkably placid and compliant babies, and Caleb certainly fit this mould. I was lulled into a sense of false security, and my confidence grew to gigantic proportions. I joined a playgroup with him when he was a tender six months, under the misguided belief that he needed to increase his social skills and would enjoy the stimulation. He may well have enjoyed the playgroup, but he certainly couldn't do or say much to indicate this. I was not deterred by the other more mature aged mothers, who brought their older children along with their babies. I was starting Caleb early and I secretly thought that these other mothers were just a bit too blasé about it all. Sometimes I even dispensed unwanted advice to them, and seriously started to question why my own mother struggled at times bringing up my two siblings and me, when it really wasn't that hard.

I can now appreciate what a tremendously hard job she had singlehandedly bringing up my elder brother, who has Asperger Syndrome, my younger sister with learning and behavioural challenges and myself – no teen-angel, I can assure you. But as a new mother, the world was still a cosy black and white one for me. It was around this time that Ben and I crazily decided to try to have another baby, bearing in mind my fertility issues; we decided to not risk waiting too long to add to our family. We didn't have to wait long either as Noah was conceived when Caleb was only seven and a half months old. Now things started to get a bit tricky, as the long forgotten pregnancy sickness I experienced with Caleb, returned. With both pregnancies I suffered from hyperemesis gravid arum (HG), a severe form of morning sickness that can last day and night.

When I was expecting Caleb, I had given up work fairly early in the pregnancy, and coped with my constant tiredness by resting. Of course the next time around I had a still very dependent small baby to attend to, and felt acutely exhausted. Some days I couldn't even keep down any fluid so would go to my doctor for an intravenous injection. This persisted until around the twenty week mark, and then began to thankfully subside. Motherhood was beginning to lose its shine about now. During one of the routine pregnancy screening tests administered, Noah was flagged as having a higher risk of having Down syndrome, than was optimum. I was offered an amniocentesis (amnio) to determine whether he may have the condition, but was explained the potential risks associated with this and the possible accidental miscarriage of the pregnancy.

Ben and I agonised over this decision, and I didn't feel equipped to handle the hard choices necessary for parenthood. Eventually we decided to go ahead with the amnio, but I was extremely nervous before this appointment. This time around I was attending a different hospital and we arrived at the appointed time, with far less bravado than during previous visits. The ECV to attempt to try to turn Caleb's breech position was discomforting, but the amnio was excruciatingly painful. Noah would not stop moving inside my uterus, and the doctor had to insert a very large needle partially and leave it there until he could safely fully insert it to extract some amniotic fluid. It was a long tense time before he could do this and his lack of confidence was obvious by the drops of sweat dripping off his forehead onto my bare stomach. To our relief he advised us that he hadn't come into contact with the baby, but that I may leak some fluid and would need to see my doctor immediately if this occurred. I was just glad it was over, and we anxiously awaited the results, which were fortunately negative for Down syndrome but they did confirm Noah's gender and thwarted my vision of the perfect "pigeon pair", one boy and one girl. My sister-in-law was expecting her first child at the time, and was immensely pleased that she was having a girl, so my competitive streak suffered a huge blow. She would go on to have her "pigeon pair", a girl and then a boy, but it just doesn't matter anymore. I wish I knew then that we would not want any other child other than our gorgeous Noah, and that these were not important things to be worrying about. Hindsight is a beautiful gift.

To say I had any control during Noah's birth would be a total lie. Once again my dreams of a triumphant natural delivery were to be obliterated. I began "spurious contractions" about three days prior to Noah's birth. These are basically bloody useless contractions that mean you get to be shunted back and forth to hospital, ridiculed by smug midwives and intimately prodded by curious doctors. Eventually they got sick of seeing me shuffling the labour ward corridors, using Ben as my walking stick, and decided that they may as well let us have this baby. I was scheduled for my waters to be broken and to be induced the next day. Let the games begin. Nine a.m. sharp, and it was *very* sharp, saw me having a large knitting needle inserted into my privates to break my waters. I know I keep saying this, but this was even more agonising than the ECV and the amnio put together! Still it was nothing in comparison to what was to come.

Immediate intense contractions, no time to put in the epidural properly so a botched job with that, whereby it was only slightly effective and I had a whopping great lower back wound that would need to be managed by the hospital's pain management team afterwards. Excuse me, but isn't the actual *hospital* meant to be the pain management team? The things you learn hey? Anyway, after six hours of wild, humiliating, naked thrashing about on the bed, Noah was born. With the help of gas, pethidine (which made me vomit repeatedly), the botched epidural, the vent house suction or the vacuum extraction as it's more aptly known, the forceps and numerous stitches, my darling was born. Noah had gotten stuck in my narrow birth canal, as is common with first time natural deliveries and I narrowly missed having an emergency C-section. He was whisked away to the neonatal ward for some oxygen immediately after the birth, but I was in no state to even register this.

Noah was actually remarkably untouched by all the drama, weighing a more robust seven pounds three ounces, and only sustaining minimal trauma. His head was a bit alien-like from the forceps, but we were used to giving birth to sons with misshapen heads by then. Ben said the room looked like a war zone, with cupboards flung open and surgical equipment strewn everywhere, but I didn't really care. Apparently there was a student doctor, who I consented to being there in my state of pre-birth calmness, who had never attended a natural birth before, and looked decidedly green by the end of it. That could have also been due to the needle stick injury we later found out he had sustained during the melee. So to complete my humiliation, I was also tested for AIDS. A very proud parental moment. I have since come across this young doctor in the paediatric emergency ward on one of my many hospital adventures for Noah's asthma, and have prayed that he doesn't recognise me. I needn't have worried; as I wasn't a writhing, swearing, screaming banshee on this particular occasion he had absolutely no recollection of who I was. It did also occur to me that he was probably more familiar with other parts of my anatomy and not my face; either that or he was extremely tactful and therefore not going to be qualified to be a paediatrician.

While on this slightly bitter note, I would like to expressly thank that kind, compassionate midwife for her particularly useful piece of advice during the height of my birthing distress – "Well Darling, if *you* won't push, that baby won't be getting *itself* out of there!" Thanks for that. This humbling experience seems to have set the tone for our lives as we now know them.

2

Noah's Difficult First Months, Asthma Related
Hospitalisation and Early Signs of Autism for Both Boys

So like a pair of stunned rabbits, we returned home from hospital with our Noah. I felt flat and disillusioned by the whole birthing process and had a monumental case of the "baby blues". It was difficult to adjust to having both a toddler and a newborn vying for our attention. I was experiencing some weird déjà vu moments mixing Noah up with Caleb because both babies looked so similar and were born so close together. We were still under the illusion that Ben could maintain some sort of stressful career back then, and he was doing long hours in the cut throat world of telecommunications. He was admirably trying to forge up the career ladder, in order to provide for our growing family and we were battling stress on several fronts. I had no plans to return to work, which was lucky as this wouldn't happen for another seven years.

My sister-in-law gave birth to her baby girl a few months after Noah was born, and I remember feeling acutely jealous that she seemed to have bounced back after her less difficult birth. We also felt drawn into a silent struggle for the extended family's support and attention. Thankfully we opted out of this tug-of-war once it became apparent that our domestic situation was going to be very different from most people's. We have had to become quite self-sufficient, but find this lessens our expectations of others and reduces our disappointment. Both of our sets of parents have their own grown children with special needs; they were also working full time and under a great deal of pressure in their personal lives. Sometimes it is hard to avoid conflict derived from sibling rivalry and unmet expectations of the grandparents' involvement with the boys. Ben and I feel ousted at times by our needier brothers and sisters, but it does help to strengthen our own immediate family unit and encourages clearer communication.

Although Noah also was a strangely placid baby during the day, he would become colicky and distressed every night. During the day he would lie in his floor bassinet, becoming fixated on the shifting lights in the room or the turning fan. I remember my sister visited when he was about two months old and Noah was just staring off into the distance with a little smile on his face, for an inordinately long time. She waved her hands in front of his face and said "*Hello!* Is there anyone there?" Then she told me how lucky I was that he was so easy going. I wasn't feeling too lucky though, as I thought he was simply exhausted from all his nocturnal activity and that was why he was so content during waking hours.

During the night he would rage and scream for endless hours, so I often retreated to the lounge with him trying not to wake Ben and Caleb. I discovered he may snatch small windows of sleep if I lay on my back with him lying flat on top of me, tummy to tummy. Then I would have to continuously rock him very vigorously up and down or he would resume screaming. We nicknamed Noah Fusspot Fidgeter, one of the more polite names we called him at the time and I began my close relationship with a physiotherapist for a slipped disc in my back that would never heal. I also became very well acquainted with late night infomercials on TV. One night Ben came out to keep me company and became so fixated with a

Tony Robbins ad that promised us we could "Unleash our Power Within", that he bought the whole expensive set of CDs. We did try to embark on the road to personal improvement, but soon came to realise that we hadn't unleashed any power at all, just my fury at having bought some rhetorical bullshit. We were becoming cynical. To prevent any more impulsive late night purchases, Ben was banished out to the rumpus room in his quest for a good night's sleep and hasn't been seen since. What a devious master plan!

Meanwhile I was still breastfeeding Noah and he had an insatiable appetite, and seeing as he couldn't scream while feeding, he got fed a lot. At an early health check with the Child Youth Health nurse, he was announced the winning record holder for weight gain within a week. I was a tearful, exhausted mess and started querying what was wrong with this baby as he was nearly six months old and was still waking hourly through the night. She suggested I wean him onto the bottle and put our names down to attend a week long in-patient program at a sleep clinic, where we would be taught the fine art of controlled crying. A subject I was to become very familiar with over the ensuing years.

I no longer had any notions of being a gold medal winning mum anymore, but consequently was a bit more popular at playgroup, and we were just in survival mode. We didn't have time to follow through on the sleep clinic plan, as Noah was also diagnosed with asthma by the time he was six months old; after he had suffered a severe case of the nasty Respiratory Syncytial Virus (RSV) that landed him in hospital and would leave him permanently susceptible to problems with his narrow airways. This wasn't his first respiratory related visit to hospital as I had taken him to the emergency ward when he was only five weeks old, with a cold and breathing difficulty. His long history of asthma related illness was beginning.

During one of his hospital stays, around seven months old, Noah slept in his barred cot with his favourite comfort blanket covering his face, not good for a respiratory illness patient I know. Then he would sway and rock his whole body and head side to side for some time before he fell into a deeper sleep. I was quite accustomed to this, and didn't think much of it at the time until a nurse walked past and stopped to marvel at the spectacle. She very kindly said "Well I *never*! I have never seen them do *that* before! He doesn't have autism, does he?" I quickly retorted that of course he didn't have autism and she retreated with a knowing smile. I thought we would have known if he had something as horrible as that, not that I had any actual idea what autism was. I assumed it was something that would be physically obvious at birth, much like Down syndrome. If only it was.

I try to remind myself of my own ignorance and lack of understanding when I am confronted by this attitude in others. I have developed a thicker skin than in those early days, but it still hurts nevertheless when people peer at your children expecting to see them sporting two heads as the evidence of their disorders. Some actually seem pissed off when they can't find any physical traits and huffily declare, "Well they look normal to me!", before storming off. The signs were there and that observant nurse's comment was to play on my mind in the following months.

Noah was assigned a paediatrician who incidentally has an autistic savant son, but his matter of fact approach was difficult to get used to. I have encountered many professionals who either have ASD themselves or family members who do, and ironically this does not seem to increase their understanding of the disorder, but rather makes them more difficult to deal with. The ones I have encountered are usually from the baby boomer generation and would not contemplate considering they may have Asperger syndrome themselves. For many, their reputation is Adelaide's worst kept secret and they are notoriously difficult to work with. Noah's first paediatrician was effective in diagnosing his chronic, persistent asthma and prescribing strong preventative medication to try to combat this, but was not receptive to the possibility of Noah having autism. He simply suggested he was "a quirky boy who may develop Attention Deficit Hyperactivity Disorder (ADHD)". Quirky doctors do not like to label quirky boys in my experience.

Despite our best efforts Noah had several hospital admissions, pneumonias, and a collapsed lung during his early years, and continues to require intensive management of his asthma. Both boys have less than optimum health and needed tonsillectomies, adenoidectomies, grommets (ear ventilation tubes), asthma and croup management from a young age. Caleb suffers from many ear infections which may have contributed to his recent secondary diagnosis of Auditory Processing Disorder (APD). Under the care of a pulmonary specialist, Noah was tested for Cystic Fibrosis which to our great relief, he doesn't have. I have read that there may be a possible link between autism and respiratory health problems in children, as so many kids I know with ASD seem to have multiple health challenges.

One of our current challenges is the necessity for Noah to wear an orthodontic plate to correct a cross-bite. As this is to align his adult teeth and is damaging them until it is rectified, we have little choice but to do this now, despite some peoples' belief that we shouldn't be subjecting him to this discomfort at such a young age. We have been advised that both boys will later require braces and I dread to think of the sensory implications of these, for Caleb especially. I will not get started on one of my disgruntled gripes about the public dental system not being geared up to cater for children with autism, meaning that as the school dental service is not equipped to manage the boys' special needs we have had to spend an exorbitant amount of money seeing specialist dentists. Unfortunately the boys' developmental delays appear to affect their dentistry also, in that they have had several adult teeth emerge well before the baby teeth have been ready to fall out, resulting in necessary, traumatic dental extractions.

Noah stayed under his first paediatrician's care for two years, and during this time I was increasingly worried about his self-imposed restricted diet as he never progressed past favouring smooth textures and bland tastes, and was beginning to display emerging repetitive rituals. He was madly into the Wiggles and started picking up any available object to use as an air guitar. He went into meltdown madness when he actually saw a real one, and smashed several of those small wooden ukuleles in true rock star fashion. I remember feeling very uneasy when I looked out of our back window to see my two-year-old holding up a large plank of treated pine from our backyard woodpile, and desperately trying to use it as a guitar. I jumped into action mode because it was about three times bigger than him and pitted with long rusty nails. Luckily Noah's reckless behaviour was cushioned by his high pain threshold, which was to become another concern as he began to throw himself off playground equipment and became covered in bruises. This behaviour coincided with his bizarre eating habits; I would have to repeat a litany of unrelated words before he would accept each mouthful of food. They were all objects he was fascinated in at the time "guitar, clock, glasses", etc. Noah needed to be served the same food, in the same bowl with the same spoon; each time or else he wouldn't eat.

He has progressed to a slightly wider range of age appropriate foods, but is still significantly limited in what he will eat. Noah will even object to the aromas of what most people identify as pleasant smelling foods such as pancakes with maple syrup and he especially dislikes the smell of any peeled citrus fruits. He has a low tolerance for any new tastes, textures and most cooking smells. He does not eat any fruit, vegetables, chicken, meat, fish or much protein at all, and will only drink water and sometimes chocolate milk. This can be very common for people with ASD and Caleb is only marginally better with his food preferences.

Both boys require dietary supplements as they suffer from anaemia and Noah has bowel problems. Prior to Noah's diagnosis I didn't realise this was consistent with ASD and nearly went crazy trying to find out why we were having so many food problems. Of course he was labelled a "fussy eater" and I was then bombarded with tough love strategies to "starve him out" and recipe books suggesting I hide his vegies in chocolate. That would be good if Noah ate the chocolate in the first place, as he didn't even eat lollies, chips, ice cream or any other kids' favourites until very recently. Even now these do not often appeal to him and he prefers salty, crunchy textures. The helpful paediatrician suggested that "if Noah lived in my house then he would have to eat sushi like the rest of us". Ben and I love sushi but I can't see Noah chowing down on some nice tasty sashimi, any time soon. I keep telling myself that it's OK for Noah to have cheese balls for breakfast and at least he doesn't insist on eating those using toothpicks, like Dustin Hoffman's character in *Rainman*. As he has now expanded his biscuit repertoire to include BBQ shapes, Pizza Shapes, Chicken Crimpies and Jatz consumed by the box full at a time, they sit on the kitchen windowsill resembling an Arnott's criminal line-up of biscuit boxes.

These developmental differences were one of the key drivers motivating me towards an autism diagnosis for Noah. He failed to meet several of his milestones in comparison to Caleb's timeline for these. This served to cement the idea for us that Caleb was our "normal" one and that Noah was a bit different. We absolutely loved both boys equally, and Noah was a funny, affectionate and clever little character, but we were uneasy about his development. Caleb, however, was flying under the radar and had also developed speech issues whereby his articulation was delayed and he began to have a fairly severe stutter. He commenced seeing a speech therapist and had his first set of grommets inserted into his ears. He is now on set three and when I asked the Ear Nose and Throat (ENT) specialist how many he might be likely to need, the ENT informed me that he had inserted thirteen sets into one patient of his who had Down syndrome. I hope this will be last set for Caleb.

The subject of speech in children with autism can be a source of competition and controversy amongst parents and practitioners. It can become the yardstick for autism severity, creating confusion and misunderstanding. We are fortunate that our boys can express themselves via speech; although they often rely heavily on visual aids also such as daily schedule charts to effectively do this. There are days, however, when their speech patterns begin to feel like someone is tapping on your forehead with a tiny hammer, all day long. They also have the ability to vocally tantrum and verbally refuse to comply with requests. Are we grateful for their communicative abilities? Yes of course, but they too have their challenges.

They both enjoy engaging in "verbal perseveration" at times. This is the nerve fraying practice of repeating phrases to each other, almost in a role-playing manner. Sometimes it is like a switch is flicked, signalling the beginning of a nightmarish linguistic loop, often about the most inane and boring subject, or their current favourite game is to repeat whole episodes of *The Big Bang Theory* to each other. To witness, it's liked being trapped in a bad *Monty Python* movie, and often occurs when we are all captive in the car. Many people with ASD will engage in various forms of self-stimulatory practices, or "stimming" as they are commonly called. These can be in the form of stereotypical behaviours such as hand-flapping or body rocking, sometimes lining up objects or spinning wheels on toys. They appear to be ways for people with ASD to neurologically "re-set" themselves and to self-regulate their behaviour. Often Caleb and Noah even annoy each other with their forms of "stimming", resulting in some vicious feuds.

After six years of speech therapy for Caleb, he now only has mild articulation and stuttering issues that mainly surface when he is anxious. His primary issue is now the rapid rate of speech he uses, as his brain processes information very quickly and he tries to keep up with his speech. He can still be difficult to understand at times, especially when there is little context to his conversations. Noah also started to see the speech therapist for severely delayed speech sound issues; he was virtually unintelligible until past the age of four when we embarked on an intensive program to rectify this.

Happily he has made amazing progress in this area and we are immensely relieved. Both boys have fairly pedantic language styles and Noah tends to speak in a repetitive monotone, as his speech processes are slower than typically developed children's. This can become quite tiresome as he usually sticks to his current obsession as his conversational topic. He also likes to endlessly question and repeat phrases to confirm his understanding, and then often needs you to repeat that same phrase back. He sometimes will only talk using echolalia, the very annoying habit of repeating exactly what you say to him, back to you. This made me so crazy one day that I said to Ben as a joke, "What did one autistic boy say to the other?", and Ben dutifully replied, "What?", and my answer was "What did one autistic boy say to the other?" Slightly derogatory and stereotypical I know, but it broke the tension that day.

Caleb has more sophisticated language, but will pedantically correct you if you use a word that differs from his preferred descriptive term: he does not understand that there are many ways of saying the same thing, and gets quite agitated by this. They will both take you very literally, so we have learnt to be precise with our speech – there are no "laters, in a moments, soon or maybes". To get technical, they will probably always struggle with the semantics and pragmatics of speech – that is the more social use of language and its practical applications.

I have become quite adept at tag team therapy for the boys; sometimes they even attend the same sessions, although that can be a white-knuckle experience. Often I have to mentally remind myself which boy I need to take to which health professional and I can proudly say I have never taken the wrong one yet! Taken the wrong notes and information? Yes absolutely. When I was at the height of my fact finding mission regarding Noah's unusual behaviour, one naive speech therapist fresh out of university suggested that Noah couldn't possibly have autism. Her theory was that Noah's developmental problems were due to my penchant for matching clothes and accessories, thus causing him to have inherited some kind of obsession gene, and that if I just relaxed about it all then he would be fine. I have heard different variations of this theme since, but none directly linking their autism to my sartorial choices.

3

Noah's Autism Diagnosis

I was getting close to desperation with handling Noah's issues, when I met a new friend at playgroup. I was sick of being patronisingly reassured by the GPs, paediatricians and speech therapists that everything was fine and I was convinced that my instincts were right; at that stage I was thinking Noah had ADHD. A new mum at playgroup had a son a bit older than Noah who had quite severe autism. He didn't have the ability to communicate via speech and had many visibly stereotypical autistic traits, he constantly bounced, handflapped and shrieked, making little eye contact and only showed interest in his very narrow areas of obsession. I thought it was exceptionally brave of her to bring him out to our group, but now realise that she was just getting on with her life, as you do. We got talking about Noah and she very tentatively suggested, "I know he's not like Michael (*name changed*), but do you think he could have autism?" I thought, "Autism! Again there's that word. Hmmm I had better go and think about this."

So I went and researched, I Googled and noticed that autism popped out at me from everywhere: the TV, and every magazine and newspaper I read. I still was unsure as the diagnostic criteria is so varied, and with Noah being only two years old it was really hard to determine what was typical toddler behaviour and what was abnormal. But I started to suspect that he might have some disorder like this, so the following week my friend gave me the details of an innovative Adelaide psychologist who specialised in the early detection of autism. I will never forget what doors that information opened up for us.

At the time, there were few diagnostic avenues to explore in Adelaide and little standardisation of procedures. Since then the processes have become formalised and more practitioners are qualified to diagnose childhood autism, hopefully making the journey easier for some families. I feel compelled to share my knowledge and experience when asked to, in order to repay the support I received in those early days. The autism community generally is a close knit group: with Adelaide being a smaller city with fewer resources than others in Australia, we rely heavily on shared information among parents. I am always willing to talk to new families about services and early intervention education; I find this gives greater meaning to our challenges.

Luckily the psychologist we met is one of the worldwide leaders in autism detection and diagnosis. She is doing some ground breaking work in the field of diagnosing children as young as one to two years old, using a new diagnostic tool she has developed. She has also founded an early intervention program here, using strategies based on principles of Applied Behavioural Analysis (ABA), proven to be an effective behaviour modification program. She is well respected and thankfully her diagnoses are recognised as being definitively accurate, leaving little room for contention. Naturally I was mistaken in my prediction of an ADHD diagnosis (although autism is often misdiagnosed as ADHD initially) and Noah was diagnosed at the age of two years and four months with autism. We were thankful to get such an early diagnosis and immediately became eligible for a placement within this psychologist's intervention program, which we accepted.

It was to be a steep learning curve for our family, with admission into the program on the proviso that I would undertake at least fifteen hours a week of one to one therapy with Noah for twenty weeks. The basic theory of the program is based on operant conditioning under the premise that a child's brain is at its most elastic and best able to receive new information before the age of five, therefore new skills can be taught, positive behaviour reinforced and undesirable behaviour replaced with maximum success during this stage of development. Evidence suggests, however, that new skills can be taught at any age and can be beneficial for people with ASD as certain pathways linking the neurons in the brain may be damaged in people with autism, and that these can sometimes be repaired by modifying behaviour and thought. Positive behaviour is rewarded with any motivating reward for that child such as food or a play with a favourite toy, but is gradually phased out into more intrinsic rewards such as verbal praise and smiles. That is a very simplistic explanation, but this appears to be the only therapy for autism that has clinically proven results.

We were trained initially in a clinic with several senior therapists and then the program became home-based, with regular input from a coordinator. We completed the program and taught Noah basic skills such as using gestures like waving, pointing, nodding and shaking his head to augment his communication. We played structured games to facilitate turn taking and sharing, and to stimulate his imagination. These are usually deficits in children on the spectrum. We also taught him more concrete skills such as his colours, alphabet, numbers up to twenty, and gender recognition, discovering that he has a formidable memory.

This was quite a commitment as I documented my results in

the prescribed format and had a consultant therapist visit regularly to oversee and individualise our goals. A lot of the work was done in a formal table top teaching setting to minimise distractions and elicit compliance from Noah. Caleb inadvertently benefited from this therapy also as he sat in on our sessions, but it was tricky managing him vying for my attention at the time. He often used to engage in inappropriate behaviours like crawling under the table and pretending to be a cat, which the visiting therapists observed carefully, often with a raised questioning eyebrow.

The boys' hyperactivity was reaching uncontrollable new heights making it difficult for Ben or me to manage if we both weren't present. Caleb would usually instigate this, due to his need to lead and control his environment, and Noah would follow, making them impossible to calm down. Most specialists will not suggest that a sibling may have autism unless directly approached by the parent with a concern. Needless to say, there were a few relieved professionals out there when Caleb was eventually diagnosed a couple of years later. The early intervention program probably helped *us* to learn techniques and strategies to deal with both boys, just as much as it taught them pre-school skills. It can be difficult for children with ASD to generalise and transfer their skills to different settings and this was certainly the case with Noah. As he aged, his autism became more entrenched and apparent, so we had varied results at his final evaluation. Despite this, I consider us very fortunate to have had the opportunity to participate in such a valuable and high quality program.

The diagnosing psychologist argued that Noah clearly had autism in her opinion, and not simply a language disorder causing his behaviours, and therefore should be diagnosed as such. We agreed wholeheartedly as there is no worse place than living in "limbo land" on the autism spectrum. These professional disputes are very common when dealing with doctors, teachers, speech therapists and all the other multi-disciplinary practitioners involved in an autism diagnosis. There are still so many myths needing to be debunked surrounding what presentation a person with autism may have.

Until recently Noah had a small amount of a commonly prescribed anti-psychotic medication to assist with his anxiety and motor tics, it also stimulated his appetite to lessen the impact of his eating habits. This worked quite well for him and it had noticeable benefits for a time, however we began to suspect it was masking problem behaviours and interfering with his all-important bowel movements. So it's au naturel for him too, I'm afraid.

I believe that parents can only determine whether medication is appropriate for their own children, and not any others. It is hard enough evaluating this with the help of a practitioner for our own children, without making that judgement call for others; although this does not seem to deter some people from feeling compelled to give uninformed and unwanted advice. Medication may work well for one child and not for another and can have extremely varied results. I know plenty of parents that choose to medicate themselves and not their children with autism, as so many parents suffer from long-term anxiety and depression.

4

Caleb's Challenging Behaviours, Autism
Diagnosis and Psychological Therapy

As Caleb approached the age of four, I began to hear that niggling voice of concern again and could no longer ignore his erratic behaviour. Both boys became heavily reliant on comfort objects during their toddlerhood, and in a pre-emptive strike I replaced their dummies with small cut up pieces of flannelette sheets or "blankies" as we called them, ever mindful of their speech issues. Caleb immediately began to stuff his right to the back of his mouth and chew it all day long, and they would end up soaking wet, emitting a truly revolting smell. So I started a "blankie" factory and would cut up several identical sheets into small portions, blue for Caleb and yellow for Noah. These would be taken everywhere, Noah would sleep with his over his face as previously described and Caleb would leave sodden ones stashed around the house. It was all working beautifully until the mean old speech lady advised us to completely get rid of Caleb's, as they were impairing his speech just as much as a dummy would.

I could certainly see her point of view, but broke out in a light sweat just contemplating this process. She suggested we give them all to "the blankie fairy" to take away in a bag one night and give to a smaller needier boy than Caleb. Excellent, we did *just* that. So with my resolve hardened we put the bag outside the back door and made a fuss of showing Caleb and telling him they would be gone later. As we didn't attempt this overnight but in the morning, I then distracted him for a while and whipped them off to the waiting wheelie bin. All good so far. Once the Bob the Builder DVD finished he wandered off into his room looking for good old "blankie". I brightly reminded him that they had gone to the fairy so let's just move on and go out to the park, away from the scene of the crime. No, he wasn't having that and insistently started gibbering and pointing up to the cupboard where I used to keep the spare supply of "blankies" telling me to get another one out for him. I tried to move him on; he started escalating to a full on tantrum, or meltdowns as we now call them. He began to cry and stamp his feet, before resorting to rolling on the ground in hysterics.

This was Caleb digging his heels in, and I was still confident he would get over it, so I just went about my business for a while. Well, he raged all day, all night and solidly for the next three days. I nearly caved in on around day two before the wheelie bin was emptied, but then reminded myself we would have to do it all over again, not to mention having to wash the smelly buggers, so I then tearfully rang the trusty parent helpline for a good talking to. Caleb was like a drug addict looking for a fix and he would circle around the cupboard screaming for his "bwankie" so that we felt like the worst parents ever. Eventually after a week or so his withdrawal symptoms lessened and there was only the occasional "blankie" related meltdown, so by the time we next went to speech therapy and I was asked how the weaning went, I could happily say, "Yeah, no worries at all." They say never to argue with an Aspie as you won't win, but ha ha, I won that one! Like I had any choice in the matter.

Lots of children with autism are keen on carrying objects around with them. Our friend Michael from playgroup used to have a toothbrush in each hand and I don't think this was to keep on top of his dental hygiene; he just liked the feel of them. Another boy I know would turn up at the Autism SA pre-school development program with a rubber toilet plunger (I sincerely hope unused) in his hand, but he also had the foresight to wear rubber gloves too. Less user-friendly perhaps than the toothbrushes, but he may have had aspirations to be a plumber. And then you just get the downright dangerous, like the beautiful ruby jewelled metal letter opener that we found in Caleb's pocket recently. Lovely.

When Caleb wasn't so fixated with his "blankie" he began to play more with other toys, but to my increasing frustration, I noticed he also began to take them all apart. Caleb was very adept with a screwdriver from a young age, and now has his own real tools in Ben's tool shed. It's just easier that way. So I would find all the components of his toys strewn around the house and yard; due to his short attention span he couldn't be bothered to put them back together. This was often done in the blink of an eye, sometimes even in the car from the way back from the toy shop, and when asked about why he did this he would innocently reply, "I just wanted to see how they work"; you can't argue with that, I suppose.

I have yet to see a pen given to him that has remain unscathed by his compulsion to disassemble it; invariably they all end up reduced to useless coils and nibs, never to be usable again. When we visit the pen-loving paediatrician, it's like "Clash of the Aspies". Caleb would also get lengths of rope and tie up elaborate pulley systems around his outdoor swing set, impressive but slightly unusual I thought. I began to be uncomfortably reminded of my brother, who would do these same things as a boy, and progressed to taking apart the family TV sets and VCRs when we weren't looking. I once went to set my old fashioned style bedside alarm clock, only to discover it missing and in a pile of springs and bells under his bed. He too, wasn't very interested in reassembling the items.

I love my brother, but we have all had a difficult relationship with him at times. He is a unique, eccentric individual who has not conformed to any mainstream standards, often living the life of a drifter chasing his thwarted ideals, causing untold worry to my mother. He was diagnosed as a boy with having a genius level IQ and has amazing recall, visual perception, mechanical and technical abilities, not to mention his enviable drawing skills. These artistic traits run in our family with Mum being a watercolour artist and Noah displaying a love and aptitude for drawing. But my brother has struggled for his whole life to relate to people, making poor choices concerning his own children and immediate family. We go for very long periods of time without contact, as he gravitates towards remote rural places, at one stage to pursue his love of building eco-domes for disadvantaged communities. I don't think he would mind me saying that there is an expression that in every family there is a "mad uncle", and that our boys are fortunate enough to have *three* of these.

Nowadays Caleb is enjoying more sophisticated interests favouring the areas of science and technology. He loves his computer, I-Pad, Nintendo DS and WII games, but is just as interested in sparkly gems, soft toys (especially cats) and silky fabrics. He also dabbles in the classic Aspie areas of astronomy, dinosaurs, insects and chemistry. He does have strong obsessions, but is a bit of an all-rounder with other interests, and his emerging fascination with weapons is a concern. He has become a crack shot with his Nerf guns, shooting out foam darts with deadly accuracy. One day he launched a dart at high speed at our big TV screen where it stuck at an unreachable height, with the TV being up high, supposedly out of harm's way. Anyway, Noah went into an immediate meltdown as he was engrossed in watching a show, so my blood pressure shot up and I snapped at Caleb, "Get that down right now!", not quite knowing how he would manage this. He ignored me and launched another dart directly at the TV; I didn't even register where it landed before I shouted at him, "Caleb! I said *not* to do that again!" He calmly looked at me and in a withering tone said, "Well I got it down, *didn't I?* "And he had done just that, with one well aimed shot he had dislodged the first dart. Bloody hell.

He has also made an uncannily effective cross bow out of his plastic boomerang, a plastic shovel handle (sans its head) and a skipping rope. It too launches Nerf dart missiles, usually at point blank range into our faces. Another favourite pastime is playing with these plastic coated short lengths of magnets called Magnetix, and as they come with magnetic balls he makes all kind of domes and pyramids out of them. Sometimes we walk into the lounge room and he has magnetised a small piece onto every single exposed nail head on our wooden floorboards. The whole room is set up like a booby trap and God help the person who steps on one or tries to move any. Instant detonation – of *Caleb* that is. Caleb is fond of lining objects up, like many kids with autism, but doesn't like them to be tampered with. Every situation can be a learning experience for his inquisitive little brain, in the bath he likes separating the bubbles from the water with plastic cups and bottles: "Doing a *sciencefic* experiment Mum. Separating the water from the *molecools*". Of course.

It was clearly time to put in another call to our trusty diagnostic psychologist Rachel. This time I arrived at her office with Caleb, a month before his fifth birthday, and she took one look at him, greeted him with "Hello Caleb", and was met with no eye contact or any response from him. She lifted an eyebrow at me and asked, "What are you thinking Rochelle?" I answered, "Asperger's?" And she replied "Yep. Looks like it". She had Caleb's background information and history, and his diagnosis was conclusive as Caleb clearly met the criteria for Asperger syndrome. Interestingly enough he actually met the criteria for autism, due to his early language difficulties, but Rachel felt his presentation was more in keeping with Asperger's. We agreed with this, but Caleb did cross over into some extreme behaviours and sensory problems, that were more in autism territory at times. He also met the criteria for ADHD, as do many people with ASD, but this would not have been a sufficiently accurate diagnosis. Rachel explained that so often Asperger syndrome is mistaken for ADHD and misdiagnosed, causing frustration for many families. This ADHD component of Caleb's physiology makes him very resistant to traditional relaxation and psychological therapies, as we were to discover.

Caleb would go on to have a long, chequered history with psychologists – or "psychos" as we jokingly refer to them depending on their level of competence; with some successes and some absolutely woeful experiences. We can usually gauge upon entering a room whether the therapist will have the upper hand with him, or whether he will eat the person alive. He has recently been assessed by a school appointed psychologist as having an IQ in the gifted range. We were not jumping for joy with this news as it only confirmed what we already knew, that is that yes he *is* smarter than us. That was another instance of the diagnosing professional having undiagnosed Asperger syndrome himself. I particularly appreciated that in his detailed report, it was noted that Caleb faced the testing psychologist giving no eye contact whilst sitting on a *forty five degree angle*. Those are the vital pieces of information we need to know. The interpretation of the tests they administer can be tricky at the best of times. I have simplified this by supplying them with my own descriptions such as the Welcher (the Wechsler) followed by the Whoopsy (the WPPSI) and then you'll need a strong Whisky (that'll be the WISC).

One poor unfortunate psychologist, who visited the house, was fired up with a burning passion to practise some relaxation methods he had been trained on at a high profile autism conference. So he came armed with his briefcase, laptop and his lovely calm persona, ready to tackle some of the difficulties we were having. Firstly he explained the process to us, and then he began to demonstrate the individual muscle relaxation process with me. The psychologist was trying to prepare Caleb, so he would know what to expect when it was his turn, but Caleb continued to do his usual jumping bean impression, tearing from couch to couch, throwing cushions in his wake. It was my turn now to sit back and watch the magician at work, as he firstly wrestled Caleb for the TV remote in an effort to turn off the TV, before he settled on just turning down the blasting volume. Then he tried to gently manoeuvre Caleb into a comfortable position on our not so clean floor rug, but Caleb kicked him in the face, so he wisely kept a bit more distance between them. Next he tried to slowly massage Caleb's hand but Caleb bit his arm, *hard*. Then he thought he might just change tack, as good psychologists do, and would give Caleb some deep pressure that we knew he loved. So he tried to wrap Caleb in one of the weighted quilts we use at home to calm the boys, but Caleb buried himself in it with all the cushions on top, and wouldn't come out for the duration of the session.

It was only once the poor man retreated and convinced Caleb that he was finished trying to "relax" him that Caleb emerged from his cocoon. I thought the psychologist was really graceful, only gritting his teeth slightly, while Caleb then unpacked his briefcase, took apart his pens, and played with his laptop. He cleared his throat as I tried to wipe the smirk from my face before he announced, "Well this technique doesn't work for everyone. Next time we might try something different with Caleb". Indeed. Thankfully Caleb is now seeing a very astute psychologist, specialising in treating school aged boys with Asperger's. He passed the "Keeping Caleb in Control Test" on our very first visit, only once being tripped up when he told Caleb he would be with him in "just a minute". Well it was about three minutes, but as he has never made that mistake again, he was allowed that minor indiscretion. The psychologist James (*name changed*), spends time building a rapport with his clients, and interacts with the kids individually while the parents wait in the waiting room, for a portion of the session. He is also not afraid to give the concrete, specific advice which we need, and not waste our time with stressful relaxation techniques.

5

Both Boys' Kindergarten year, Noah's Toileting Issues and Broken Arm, and Caleb's Gastro Hospitalisation

I was more than ready for Noah to begin his kindergarten year by the time he was four years old, but was less confident about his readiness, due to his lagging self-help skills and delayed speech acquisition. He had attended a special pre-school development program run by Autism SA, where the focus was on preparation for kindy and school, but we remained apprehensive about this. Caleb had attended a different local kindergarten from the one Noah was to, after having Caleb's kindy staff heavily dispute his diagnosis. They weren't asked to be involved in the diagnostic process as they had already adamantly indicated that Caleb was developing typically, in their expert opinion. Despite such obvious signs like his obsession with making an identical missile launcher each and every morning without fail, using toilet rolls, and going into meltdown mode on the rare occasion that he wasn't able to. There were also other indicators, one being the more obvious tendency he had to attempt to control his peers in elaborate fantasy role play games, mimicking his current video game obsession. He still does this to the extent that he scripts his friends' and Noah's responses for them, becoming agitated when they don't follow his rules for the game.

Due to Caleb's older age, and ongoing speech and sensory issues, I was more confident this time that he had an ASD. Like Noah's diagnosis though, it was still very early to detect Asperger syndrome and we would come across many non-believers. Both boys were to attend the local public primary school, within close walking proximity, as we thought this was a good place to start with their schooling. We were aware that like many of our friends, this may not be our last school decision, as many families move from school to school, trying to find a better educational fit for their children with ASD.

Caleb was already attending transition visits there when he was diagnosed; we didn't want to consider alternative options for him as the local school was welcoming of the boys' attendance there. We are fairly limited here in Adelaide anyway. We have public or private schools, or could apply to attend a special school which we did not feel would suit Caleb's needs. There is much anticipation surrounding the possibility of autism specific classes or schools being established in the near future, of which we are in dire need here.

Noah's schooling, on the other hand, was causing us some indecision, as we worried more about his ability to adapt to a mainstream school setting. He was toilet trained to urinate in the toilet, but until the age of seven-and-a-half refused to sit on the toilet to do his bowel movements. Despite extensive occupational therapy targeting this issue, he was unable to do this, and required a nappy for his bowel movements. Fortunately, or unfortunately, I am not always sure, he has constipation most of the time due to his iron supplements and restricted diet and he can simply hold on to his bowel movements for days, if he chooses to. Therefore he would very politely whisper to us in the evening (usually at precisely the same time each day, or every few days) "Poo Mummy" or "Poo

Daddy" if *I* was really lucky. So we would take him into his room, shut the door, pop his nappy on and leave for a few minutes before we got another polite "Ready Mummy" or "Ready Daddy" if *Ben* was really *unlucky*. Then the nappy got changed, and I took the trouble to flush the contents down the toilet taking the toilet training expert's advice. Ben didn't bother, preferring to stink out the wheelie bin, then we would wash our hands and off we went.

Noah was scared of sitting on the toilet seat and he always stood to urinate, even from a very young age. We had experts visit, watched DVD's targeted at toileting help for children with disabilities and tried umpteen different desensitisation methods. Noah really enjoyed watching the DVD and it became one of his favourite bedtime cartoons over the years, and the rest of us loved sitting on our super comfy padded toilet seat, but Noah just politely kept saying "No thanks" to our offers to try it. We tried some more high pressure campaigns to entice him to try, usually resulting in distress (ours) and constipation (his) for several days, and had resigned ourselves to the status quo, much like Noah's eating regime.

One hilarious stand-out innovation was Ben's idea to cut out holes in Noah's nappy and persuade him to sit on the toilet, hoping he would poo through the nappy hole. Trying to smother our giggles we did manage to get one of those nappies onto Noah, before he took off running around the house, laughing hysterically. His bare bottom resembled a rare baboon species, rendered particularly eye-catching by the white fluff it was shedding from the nappy lining and the red texta "target" that Ben had drawn to guide his cutting out. We eventually resorted to having several small adult size cloth nappies made to order for us by a company specialising in manufacturing incontinence products, as we simply ran out of options for Noah. We would use expensive "pull-up" pants at night for him, but as his bowel movements were so solid, it was easier and less costly to wash a lined cloth nappy each time.

Frustratingly Caleb had to tolerate the "disgusting" smells that wafted from Noah's room during his ablutions, and we were used to having those smells cling to our fingers if Noah had done a "beauty" on the Poo-ometer. While it is unusual for a seven-year-old not to be fully toilet trained, in the world of autism this was all very normal, which we found somewhat reassuring. Once we enlisted James the psychologist's help, progress was dramatic and swift. James explained that although Noah was a fairly challenging case, it can sometimes help when someone outside of the family unit is involved. This was achieved by the means of a simple reward chart with a "tick" given for each attempt (on James' special rubix-cube -shaped note paper), and an agreed target to be reached prior to the next visit. After a bit more anxiety and some further persuasion, we now do not have a single nappy in the house anymore!

We can only surmise that Noah was developmentally ready to take this monumental step, as previously we had several tantalising glimpses of success. This has truly changed our lives and Noah is so proud of himself. We are hoping to emulate some of this progress with Noah's eating issues, but James has explained that there are more sensory obstacles with this, and that it will require a different tactic to the incredible "nappy strategy". We will keep at it, as Noah does seem especially keen to please his favourite therapist, and is slowly beginning to try some slightly varied foods. We will begin to tackle the bottom wiping process, but we wouldn't want to miss out on those "disgusting smells" *too* much. We might also work on the puddles Noah leaves on the toilet floor, after just about every visit he makes, although he does succinctly articulate that " I didn't wee on the actual toilet *floor*, just on the toilet *seat*". I have spied on his technique and it is no wonder he needs some target practice when he bolts in there at a hundred miles an hour, leaves the light off and the seat down, and barely whips out his tiny little pecker before waving it all around and leaving. And let's be honest, Caleb and Ben aren't much better at it.

If Noah was a poo-er, then Caleb was definitely a spew-er. He was notorious for picking up gastroenteritis easily; without any warning he would projectile vomit, giving us our first clue he was ill. At one stage he was hooked on eating tinned spaghetti, which I was thrilled about and would be again if he were to resume eating this now defunct favourite and every time he vomited it would be after having this for dinner. It would also be either while he was in his bed, the car or on my lap, as is usually the way. On one occasion he was a lot more seriously ill than usual, and I worriedly took him down to the emergency room as he was becoming dehydrated, only to be advised that he would be fine and to return home. I set him up on the couch to rest and over the next few hours became increasingly worried as he wouldn't drink and his temperature rose; he became listless and wouldn't rouse – all the symptoms of severe dehydration. I didn't hesitate to return to the ER, more panicky than previously.

This time when another doctor saw him, she took one look at him and asked, "Is he asleep now?", I tearfully replied "No, this is how he has been for a while, but I can't wake him". She immediately told the nurse to get the IV equipment set up to start the rehydration process, but they couldn't find a vein due to Caleb's severe dehydration. A surgeon was called in and she gently explained to me that usually they would anaesthetise the IV site first, but because of Caleb's unconsciousness he wouldn't even feel the needle, which was accurate as he didn't flinch or stir at all during its insertion. This doctor's obvious skill and expertise began to reassure me but she did sharply ask "Why wasn't he brought in earlier?" to which I replied that I had but was sent home, and she tactfully didn't comment about her less professional colleagues. Caleb was admitted with severe dehydration, estimated to be ten per cent of his body weight, which was very serious in a child. He had Rotavirus and we were therefore isolated in a private room in the paediatric ward. I valiantly tried to ignore my own churning stomach and gurgling bowels as I fought the illness myself.

Many times I have been at that hospital with my children, sharing a version of their particular ailment, making for some challenging care giving. Ben would stay home with the other boy, quarantining them if the illness was contagious, as I didn't want them visiting the gastro ridden hospital ward unnecessarily. We often went in for a respiratory related issue only to return home with gastro as well. During that particular night I was awakened by a bodily function type explosion from Caleb and I sat bolt upright in my camp bed to witness him literally spray the walls with diarrhoea. Ah shite, it was a poo-mergency!

Thankfully my poor sick boy was not coherent enough to register much distress at this, but I promptly rang the nurses' bell as I was a bit freaked out. The nurse opened the door, glanced at the bed and took off again at pace to bring in a reinforcement. They efficiently donned rubber gloves and masks, got down to the work of stripping the bed, wiping the walls and floor, and then sponge bathing Caleb. I offered to help in my increasingly queasy, debilitated state, and they astutely advised me to stay where I was, on dry land. My mouth must have been set in a permanent "O" during the whole experience as once they had bundled the sheets off to the linen baskets (or hazardous waste receptacles for all I know) they sent me off in search of a good hot cup of tea, down to the parents' kitchen. I dazedly went off trying to find the rubbing alcohol, or something stronger than tea to drink, but was out of luck.

News sure travels fast in that place because a group of bored night shift nurses were gathered around their softly lit desk whispering and glancing at over at me "And there's poor Mum now. We have never seen one do *that* before ...". Another good night out on the town, but most importantly Caleb did recover without any lasting consequences, but I am not so sure about my own resulting mental health issues.

It was around this time that the pressure got to me and I hit a rebellious streak, so at the ripe old age of thirty-five I went and got my first tattoo. I decided on quite a bold blue butterfly design on my lower back, symbolising personal freedom with the blue reminding me of the boys. When I had enthusiastically drawn up my own design I hadn't anticipated the four hours procedural time, and how nervous I would be. Once my adrenaline kicked in, I nearly passed out and then had to be revived with a can of Coke, as it looked likely I would be left with a tiny pathetic black mark tattooed onto my back, at that stage. Anyway I pulled myself together, and went onto love the finished result. So much that I was back shortly afterwards; with a similar matching butterfly design for my foot, where I could better see it. I don't regret these as I now have one butterfly each for Caleb and Noah, but I do warn the boys and my school students about the pitfalls and the permanency of tattoos.

Meanwhile Noah's eating and toileting delays significantly contributed to my worry about him going to kindy. As it happened he had a wonderfully nurturing kindy staff, and I became particularly close to one special teacher there. She was endlessly patient and kind, with not just Noah but with me also, as we negotiated the ups and downs of another year. She understood that we came as a package deal, and that sometimes I cracked under the pressure. As

Caleb was on the same campus, I became a regular fixture coming and going to the school that year, sometimes making three or four trips in one day, if the boys had a therapy appointment. Noah also was only doing half day kindy sessions, as he couldn't manage a full day, so I felt constantly rushed and stressed out.

When Noah was at kindy though, I could rely on him being well supervised, his asthma medication being administered and his special needs met. So it was with surprise one day that I got that dreaded call to come to pick him up as he had injured his arm. Once a week a class of upper primary school kids came to spend time with the littlies as "buddies" and they would play together in the playground. This is a great way of mixing the older and younger children in the large primary school, and is standard practice throughout the grade levels. Noah had gotten a bit carried away and pushed his buddy from behind off a large gum tree log that features as a makeshift cubby in the yard. His buddy had inadvertently grabbed Noah's shirt with surprise as he turned to face him, bringing Noah down on top of him.

Noah was sitting on his lovely teacher's lap, very quiet and tearful, when I arrived shortly later. He was clutching an ice pack to his arm but obviously couldn't move it very well. A trip to the hospital (orthopaedics for a change of scene this time) and an x-ray revealed a wrist fracture, allowing Noah the honour of choosing a cool black arm cast, as his latest fashion accessory. The surgeon confirmed that the break would have been much harder to set had his teacher not had the foresight to apply the ice pack and ring me quickly, so I was grateful for her common sense. Unfortunately Noah is left-handed and that was the wrist he broke, so I helped him to write a "Sorry" card to his poor buddy who felt responsible for the mishap and had received the shock of his life. It is a dangerous business being Noah's buddy.

6

Therapies for Both Boys

Both boys began to have regular occupational therapy as well as speech therapy during Caleb's reception year and Noah's kindergarten year. The occupational therapist helped identify their fine and gross motor deficits and we developed strategies to assist with these. We worked on handwriting improvement for Caleb and the correct pencil grip for Noah, body strengthening for both boys as poor muscle tone and coordination are weaknesses, increasing their tactile and textural tolerance as well as identifying effective calming routines for them. We were perennially working on their reluctance to try new foods and Noah's toileting restrictions, but were becoming more resigned to these limitations.

Both boys love deep pressure feedback such as jumping on the trampoline and the repetitive movement of a swing. This helps to channel their hyperactivity and release some of that relentless energy. I recall seeing Sigourney Weaver's adult character in the movie *Snowcake* who has autism, relishing in the freedom of jumping on a trampoline despite her more advanced age. I too think it will be a long time before we can forgo having one, and this is a piece of play equipment that I vowed never to have, pre autistic children, due to its potential danger. Noah has such a love of deep pressure that in times of extreme stress he will say "Squeeze my head Mum!", meaning he wants me to perform a firm, safe squeeze around his skull to release some anxiety. I do not recommend this technique, or using any other deep pressure such as weighted quilts, unless you have been specifically trained by a therapist. The boys benefited from the input of Autism SA's senior occupational therapist, a dynamic, passionate woman whom I greatly respect. We discovered that Noah responds well to a good old head squeeze when his head has been done in. He also loves to be vigorously rocked and Caleb likes his fingertips being squeezed, another handy tip, that pun definitely intended.

One of Noah's favourite games is to lie him on his back while I pull his legs gently up towards the ceiling, giving him a nice big stretch, or to support his legs while he's tummy down, walking like a wheelbarrow. Once again, you need to be very mindful of fragile, developing bones though. Recently we went to a high-tech internationally acclaimed magic show organised by the Commonwealth Carer's Support service for children with disabilities and social disadvantages. The show was particularly enthralling for children on the spectrum, featuring laser lighting and loud theatrical music. There were all makes and models of families and children there, with diverse age groups. One particular row of teenage boys caught my eye, and my Aspie radar, as they were thoroughly engrossed in the show, all the while enthusiastically rocking in their seats, making their whole section shake and groove, giving new meaning to being at a "Rock Concert".

There is a myriad of therapies out there for people with ASD, and once again this is a very subjective area in which to calculate success. What works for one child may not for others, and finding reliable sound advice can be difficult. There are some unscrupulous practitioners cashing in on parents' desperation, offering ineffective, expensive and sometimes dangerous alternative therapies. We investigated bio-intervention, or dietary modification for Noah, with the premise that eliminating gluten and toxins from his diet would improve his challenging behaviours and bowel issues. This is a fairly common therapy for some to try, but didn't suit us as Noah's diet is so restricted that it is impossible to remove the gluten from it, as he would have nothing left to eat. Some practitioners then argue that this would induce him to try different foods, but all it would prompt Noah to do would be to starve himself.

It was around this time also that Noah was given an IQ test for school readiness, but his results were less conclusive than Caleb's. IQ tests are not always an accurate indication of a person with ASD's abilities and areas needing development, due to the nature of autism. A person with autism will often have outstanding skills in one area, such as visual processing, numerical skills, recall and identifying spatial patterns, with deficits in language, communication and social areas. This makes averaging the results and getting a true IQ reading difficult, as their profile is scattered with severe peaks and troughs.

This was the case with Noah's test, and it wasn't aided by the school outsourcing the assessment to an unfamiliar psychologist, who didn't bother to read his background history and needed Ben and I to interpret Noah's responses, due to his poor speech capabilities. Noah was obsessed with wearing lens less, heavy set plastic rim Harry Potter glasses throughout his kindy year. These were virtually surgically attached to his face, and everyone was so used to them, they no longer noticed them. He wore them throughout his psych test and the observant psychologist noted at the end of the session, "I see he wears glasses, what are his vision problems?" I burst out laughing and Noah looked delighted that he had tricked the smart lady, before I acerbically pointed out that they weren't real glasses and thought to myself "As if we would put the autistic boy in such ridiculously geeky glasses!" What a cliché. It was no surprise that other psychologists have since rendered that test as void, and frustratingly Noah had to wait for the required two years before being able to have another test administered.

Anyway we have a good idea of Noah's strengths; he is proving to have many academic ones and we are aware of the areas we need to work on. It is becoming more apparent that Noah has what I can only describe as "cognitive gaps" in his reasoning, logic and problem solving. He has not been diagnosed with an intellectual disability like many others with ASD, but you cannot assume he has the same level of awareness as a typical eight-year-old and he is certainly more reckless. For example he will run across roads and car parks oblivious to any oncoming traffic; he also absconds at shops and runs on ahead causing us extreme anxiety.

Up until recently I would walk both boys to school using a large, double pram. Noah's low muscle tone and respiratory problems means he tires easily during walks and he would happily travel in the pram, while Caleb usually walked. As Noah became more aware of the curious looks and comments we attracted, and the not so subtle taunts of his peers, he became more reluctant to use the pram and would hunch over under the canopy away from prying eyes. We were quite the local spectacle with people often smiling, some laughing, many commenting, "Oh! You have lost one!" while pointing at Caleb's empty space. Some people became downright aggressive in their confused search for an absent small baby. This was often our only safe mode of transport, but Noah does now walk further distances although it is a bit like walking with an octopus. He rarely walks on the actual footpath; he will walk on the road, in the long grass next to the path or run through parks wherever possible. He also hair-raisingly kicks at broken glass even while only wearing sandals, and will often stop to pick a piece up. He grabs at thorny rose bushes, falls over repeatedly and refuses to hold our hands. Caleb engages in a slightly less dramatic version of the "octopus walk", but it usually requires both Ben and I to manage outings, especially in crowded venues.

Noah sometimes worries us with his sense of perception as he often confuses fantasy with reality. He frequently asks, "Am I real?" or "Is this real?", and once he stopped dead in the midst of crossing a busy road to ask whether that particular moment was "real". Oh yeah, it was very real when I grabbed his hand and yanked him to the footpath! It is with little wonder that I often have vivid nightmares in which I am fighting a losing battle to keep Noah safe, and where I become distraught when he is "lost". I am now quite adept at waking myself up when it gets too distressing for me to bear. He also can behave socially inappropriately and used to love running around nude with a pair of other little boys who have autism, when they came to play. Quite a sight to behold – seeing four boys aged between six and eight, Caleb included, running around starkers. We are now quite used to it, and just pour ourselves another glass of wine and double check the front door is locked.

So it was with trepidation that Noah approached his first day of primary school. The school is a large public one, and attracts a diverse range of families from varying backgrounds. There are many other students there who have special needs, due to its size and neighbouring High School, which includes a special needs unit. We thought it would be an advantage for Noah and Caleb to go from the kindy to primary school and hopefully onto that High School, all within the one campus, and that is still our plan. At the time there were a few boys at the primary school with Asperger syndrome (including Caleb), but Noah was the only one with an autism diagnosis, contributing to our worry. We investigated a private special school, attended by some friends of ours, and our decision oscillated between the two schools for a while, as there seemed to be a balance of pros and cons for both settings. We feel that we have one foot in the disability community and one foot in the mainstream one, due to the level of severity of the boys' ASD.

Noah was to have the same teacher that Caleb had the previous year, so this was some comfort for me as she was familiar with our family situation, but I was well aware that he was moving out of that small nurturing kindergarten environment into the big wide school world. I remember reading in the *Australian Autism Handbook* (an excellent publication, in my opinion) where one mother advised that if you were going to mainstream school your child with ASD, then prepare to endlessly advocate for them. As I already had one year's experience of the school system under my belt, with Caleb having finished reception, I knew this to be sound advice.

7

Early School Challenges for Both Boys

During Caleb's first year of school we discovered that despite everyone's best efforts, it really was a case of trying to fit our "diamond pegs into round holes", diamonds being Caleb's favourite shape. The school, teachers and external services such as Autism SA and Disability SA do have the boys' education and welfare at heart, but resources are stretched and it is always difficult to accommodate individual requirements in a mainstream setting. I built up a good rapport with the people whom I credit with caring for our children for more than six hours a day, recognising their efforts in this challenging task. Misunderstandings do arise, however, patience gets tested and sometimes I need to step back emotionally in order to see the big picture.

I have learnt to battle, but to pick the important battles and in order to maintain consistency to bring strategies from home to school and vice versa. I am always willing to provide resources such as visual aids from home, and volunteered my time at school before commencing my employment there. I do find our energy is best invested in tackling the major issues, without focussing too much on the more trivial aspects. It has really been a case of the boys and us all having to "HTFU" (Harden The Frig Up), a concept that doesn't always sit well with me, but is our reality nonetheless.

Ben and I both work part-time to enable us to each have careers, while dealing with the inevitable medical emergencies that arise. We have probably attained that elusive "work/life" balance, so highly prized by the chat shows – albeit precariously for our family. Sometimes it is *very* precarious, such as during the crazy times like when Noah swallowed a marble on one Christmas Eve and we had to get the paramedics out. We never found that marble even with an X-Ray taken. More distressing was when he partially severed the top of his finger in a fully shut door, and had to have it surgically reattached. That time it was the full ambulance job to hospital, and we all suffered post-traumatic shock after that one. Poor little Caleb had accidentally shut the door on Noah's finger, so he needed comforting too. Life is usually pretty action-packed around here.

I have also learnt to be proactive in facilitating a successful outcome for the boys, while weighing up the sometimes confusing information available about autism. Soon after their diagnoses we ordered Medic Alert bracelets, and then moved onto medallion necklaces. This was a bit controversial for some people, literally labelling them with ASD as well as chronic asthma for Noah, but it provided us with some peace of mind when they were around unfamiliar people or in different settings. It was an easy way for caregivers to realise that the boys have ASD and therefore may need some accommodations regarding this, without relying on the boys' verbal skills to communicate this when they were younger. When Caleb went through a stage a of not wanting to wear his, I sought some advice from Autism SA and was reassured that we were within our parental rights to insist on this if we chose, due to safety and health concerns. Once I discussed this with Caleb and assured him that when he was older he could decide whether to continue to wear his necklace or not, he concluded that he would prefer to wear it anyway. These days neither boy wears his necklace as they are more independent, and prefer to drape their necks in skull and dragon pendants acquired on eBay.

We have always been very open with the boys and they have been aware from a young age that they have ASD. Initially they were satisfied with our explanation that this would mean that they are extraordinarily good at some skills, and would need some help with others. Lately, however, both boys have begun to be frustrated with some of the challenges involved with being on the spectrum, especially their social differences, and can get quite upset at times. Caleb is particularly astute and regularly asks if we would rather "swap" him for another boy who doesn't have Asperger's. It can be heartbreaking at times for these kids, and I know from both my personal and professional life that it is imperative we constantly work at building up their self-esteem. This will deteriorate during their teenage years so it is worth doing the ground work now, in preparation for these tempestuous years.

Unfortunately the Medic Alert necklaces did not always attract attention when necessary. During Noah's early years at school he had a relief teacher one day who was not aware of his autism nor noticed his necklace. We have negotiated with the school, through Noah's Negotiated Education Plan (NEP), that he is allowed to eat a sandwich, roll or crackers at healthy fruit time in the mornings. He still does not eat any fruit, although many teachers confidently predict that they will get him eating fruit and we would love for them to achieve what we haven't been able to in eight years of intensive therapy.

Anyway Noah tried to tell the relief teacher that he would eat his sandwich instead, but he was neither assertive nor particularly coherent at that time, so she dismissed him with a "No you won't. You won't eat *anything* then!" He took that literally of course, and came home with a full lunch box that day; he didn't eat anything all day long. I rang the principal that afternoon upon discovery of Noah's untouched lunchbox and he agreed that the situation was not handled well, at all. I brought to his attention that there may have been other children in the class with allergies, which could have had dire consequences if not managed. Of course he agreed and was empathetic to Noah's needs and I conceded that this was understandable when relief teachers came into the classroom. Thankfully we now have safety nets in place, and a more structured special needs program that helps to prevent these incidents. At the time though, I managed the situation by making up a laminated "social story" stating Noah's dietary restrictions due to his autism, and stuck it onto his lunchbox lid. I also provided a larger copy, complete with pictures, to be prominently displayed in his future classrooms.

Another challenge we face is the administration of Noah's asthma medication. Obviously when he is significantly sick I don't send him to school, however for a good proportion of the year he has asthma symptoms that can be managed by regular Ventolin doses. As he has a paediatric Asthma Plan and the school promotes being "Asthma Friendly" he is entitled to attend, when he is able to. The school has a medicine bell reminding students to take their midday medication and sometimes the teacher will write Noah's name on the board to remind them to prompt Noah, other times it is assumed he can differentiate the medicine bell from all the other identical sounding bells and take himself off to the school office for treatment. There are many instances when he has returned home wheezing and coughing as he has not had his Ventolin during the day. This is an example of a situation that requires constant monitoring and some diplomatic communication with the school staff.

I think that like most parents of children with special needs, we understand the limitations and the challenges faced by mainstream school staff, but we have little choice in continuously advocating for change within this system. The school often comments on how appreciative they are of my resourcefulness and proactive responses even now in my dual role as an employee there, but I feel I tread a fine line with it all some days. I also realise that a lot of parents don't have the confidence or guidance to establish these processes, so the school staff often refer parents with newly diagnosed children to me for information.

Maintaining communication and consistency throughout a large school such as ours requires a vigilant approach. I spend a great deal of my time forwarding reports, information and emails to the staff, attempting to avoid misunderstandings due to poor communication. In the early days I donated a copy of the *Australian Autism Handbook* to the school library, to further facilitate autism awareness and education about current best practice. Naturally I don't want to tread on too many toes and be known as one of those vigilante mums that the teachers hide from under their desks when they see you coming; so I also try to convey my appreciation and regard for their expertise, support and commitment to teaching.

I remain mindful that they have a formidably difficult job teaching sometimes over thirty children in a class each day, within the constraints of DECD (Department of Children's Development) policy while keeping the parental community happy. I do not envy their positions and therefore don't like to overstep our allocated portion of their time and energy. I have the same approach to the support agencies that assist us by coming into the school and providing mediation and guidance in critical areas. So sometimes the battle is not that bloody, but is more like a silent war of attrition against the barriers of autism and not the people involved, as I prefer us being on the same team as the boys' educators.

Caleb completed six terms of reception due to his birthday falling in June, and during this time he became quite familiar and confident with the school routines; his more challenging behaviours only began to surface during Year One. We were concerned about the boys' academic abilities prior to them beginning school; especially Noah's reading and learning capabilities. This has really been the area we have least had to worry about as both boys have proven to have remarkable recall abilities, resulting in excellent reading aptitude. Noah has surprised us all by having quite exceptional literary skills, in line with children with autism who have Hyperlexia – that is above average or precocious reading ability. He has flown through his reading curriculum, and has now moved onto more advanced material, to our great joy. Caleb too excels in this area, but perhaps not quite so spectacularly as Noah.

We are so proud of these strengths in them, not in order to compare the boys to their classmates, as we have learnt that is a futile pastime, but because they will have lifelong skills helping them along the rocky road to independence. We do come across a few other parents puzzling over the boys' higher reader levels, trying to equate this to their understanding of autism, but I no longer notice that as much. They are usually the same parents who feel absolutely compelled to negate the boys' diagnosis by trying to convince us that they "seem really normal", in an attempt to figure out why our boys might be able to do some of the things their children can't. What they don't realise is that we take as much pleasure in them learning to ride their bikes, another independent skill, or even Noah tasting a lollipop or Caleb attempting to wipe his own bum, all achievements that most parents can happily take for granted with their children. Every self-help skill attempted let alone mastered, in our house becomes a cause for celebration. It is usually well documented with visual evidence in the form of a photo; both boys have their own digital cameras, or a reward chart complete with computer generated pictures.

Visual material is so important to the boys, as they often relate better to pictures than confusing words, and are quintessential visual learners. This explains their love of TV, DVDs, computers, games and in Noah's case costumes, superhero and Lego figurines. Noah's skills in these areas progressed during his first year of school, with him becoming proficient enough to become the proud owner of his very own Nintendo DS console. Both boys can now "Google" their interests on the internet as they have high literacy levels. This is closely supervised as Caleb knows our eBay PayPal password and is already an avid online shopper, a legacy he has inherited from me. Noah will use up all the printer paper and ink, printing out pictures of Lego figurines to add to his already vast personal paper trail. He adores superheroes and likes to match his DVDs to his Lego Wii and DS games all whilst wearing a full costume ensemble, usually not complete until he is wearing a mask. You have to admire his sheer thoroughness, if nothing else, but the repetitiveness of it all can drive you mental some days. He has always done this; if he is watching a DVD he will bring out any matching paraphernalia by way of costumes, figurines or pictures. And he has an impressive array of all of these.

Noah's obsessions are strong but they do change over time, he moved on from The Wiggles and guitars to superheroes like Spiderman and Ben 10, then the aforementioned Harry Potter stage, which incidentally still makes a comeback every now and then. People don't always realise that a person with ASD can have many concurrent obsessions, and some resurface at times of stress that you thought were long extinct. There are no hard and fast rules however, as some people on the spectrum may have one narrow intense obsession that will overshadow any other interests, these being as varied as the people who have them. Another point to remember, which I recall from a helpful autism seminar, is that a child with ASD can and will learn new skills, but perhaps at a slower rate than a neurotypical child. This is a simple concept, but one that is easily forgotten during frustrating times.

While Caleb can appear more aloof and less able to relate to his peers in the playground, Noah has proven to be a popular exuberant boy, with the air of the "class clown" about him. Both personas are proving to be socially challenging, for them and for us, and it is in this arena where most of their schooling issues have begun to arise. Caleb has experienced difficulty making friends and finding common ground with his classmates, probably due to his superior intellect and lack of tolerance for their imaginative play. He does like engaging in role play, but it must be on his terms with tightly scripted outcomes and without any deviation from his set theme. As other children get older and more socially confident, they will no longer be coerced into playing like this, and thus Caleb can find them retaliating by refusing to play with him. Nowadays he has quite a few like-minded friends, usually girls or less dominant boys who let Caleb take the leadership role, but he can burn them out fairly quickly with his intensity. He loves talking about gadgets and technology, and trading Yu-Gi-Oh cards with some of the kids at school, and we delight in hearing about his social successes.

Both boys find the whirlwind sea of playground activity too overwhelming most days, they have trouble physically keeping up with the other kids and finding their friends in the large yard, all wearing identical uniforms. They also experience many nasty grazes and bruises due to their "tunnel vision" and coordination issues. Caleb had one particularly speccie "shiner" on the whole side of his face, when he rushed headlong into another boy, running with his head down.

Caleb finds it hard to participate in less structured play, and welcomes indoor activities when we are able to negotiate these with the school during the times they recognise his need for a break. Cannily, he often asks for money to buy a frozen fruit juice to occupy himself during play time. He suffers on warmer days, strongly disliking feeling hot and being extremely sensitive to sensory discomforts of any kind, such as thirst, hunger and tiredness. He tends to struggle with personal organisational skills, and is constantly losing his belongings due to his distractibility. As Caleb has heightened sensory perceptions such as his sense of smell (we call him the super-sniffer as he can detect the slightest of odours) and his acute hearing, he is observing and processing much more information than an average child usually would.

At his last audio test he was confirmed as having "supersonic hearing" as described by the technician, despite also have Auditory Processing Disorder. It is not surprising therefore that both boys come home from school absolutely exhausted and begin to melt-down in an attempt to control their environments, after trying so hard all day at school. Until recently neither of them participated in any extra curriculum after-school sports or activities but we are slowly integrating these into their routines. Caleb attended a soccer clinic and both boys now enjoy playing junior cricket, in a structured and non-competitive setting. They show surprising aptitude for some sports, attributed to their innate sense of timing and keen visual perception. The highlight of attending any of Noah's cricket matches has to be when he catches a ball thrown near his groin area, and then proceeds to dramatically yell at the top of his voice "Ahhh! My nuts!" This can be heard echoing around the lovely, tranquil cricket oval, breaking the early morning serenity.

Caleb places great importance on following school rules, which of course is an admirable trait, but it means he is a perfectionist and hard on himself if he even steps slightly out of line, and he has a tendency to rush through his schoolwork competitively wanting to finish first. He also has little tolerance for the "naughty" kids at school, such as his own brother. Noah isn't really naughty; he just has a completely different temperament from Caleb's. He likes to run in a pack in the school yard, with a boisterous group of boys who love to wrestle each other, down the back of the oval away from supervising eyes. He is hyperactive in the playground, also becoming overexcited and overwhelmed by the noise and movement. He sweats profusely as he physically exhausts himself, being under-reactive to either pain, heat or his bodily needs such as thirst and hunger.

As Noah is very easily led, and has learnt his social skills by choosing one admired friend that he intensely copies, this can result in inappropriately rough play. He will change this targeted role model depending on who is available in his immediate vicinity, as he changes classes he will always seek out either a physically active or socially immature boy to copy, sometimes even another boy with special needs. He is so influenced by his chosen peer that he will mimic their dress and interests, unfortunately not their more diverse eating habits or superior social skills though. The school are now aware that often Noah doesn't realise the consequences of his behaviour, and they too are in the difficult position of needing to provide some discipline for him, in line with their handling of the other children. Noah does get many "time outs" at school, but often doesn't know or recall what they were for, and unless Caleb has handily witnessed these we are usually oblivious to the incidents surrounding them.

We try to negotiate additional playground support for Noah, but once again there are funding and resource limitations; the school does implement various routines to assist in this problem area, and we are continually trialling new strategies. As our school grounds back onto a nature trail and creek (great for a water attracted autistic child), the groundsman discovered a nest of potentially deadly brown snakes and the children were banned from playing near them. Once again my diligent spy Caleb reported to me that when he had seen Noah wandering around near the area and interrogated him about his "out of bounds" travel plans, Noah's reply was that he was "just off to visit the snakes". Noah is extremely lucky to have such a vigilant and observant older brother, as are we to have Caleb take his brotherly responsibilities so seriously.

Relations with the school reached a delicate point when I found out again via Caleb, that Noah had kicked an older boy in his groin (or his "kiwis" as Noah this time delicately phrased it, when pressed for details) resulting in this boy needing medical attention in the school sick room. Noah was being teased and he couldn't find a yard duty teacher to assist him to manage his anger, so it was really hard to explain to Noah the inappropriateness of his behaviour. Of course we instil that there is never any excuse for physical retaliation, but try telling that to a child with autism who is left unattended to manage his own anger and distress. Sadly, this type of playground behaviour is becomingly increasingly common-place for Noah, as he gets older and the social gap between him and the other children widens.

It is common for children with ASD to invest so much into fitting into their school settings and reserving their more extreme and noticeable behaviours for home, thus causing external caregivers to question the validity of their diagnosis. This is an area that requires continual education and it becomes tedious justifying the seemingly lack of control that we have over our boys at home, when it is not apparent at school. It is always a balancing act determining what I call the "accountability versus disability" puzzle.

Noah has picked up some undesirable swear words, to be expected by his age and surprisingly not discovered earlier. Caleb and Noah have never really realised the shock value of a good swear word, and the worst they have ever tentatively experimented with has been "shit", but quickly lost interest when it didn't achieve its desired effect. So Noah has resorted to inventing his own insults which are currently "Chicken, fat, nuts, shit!" repeated emphatically and randomly, with no context whatsoever. Caleb on the other hand heard his Dad once say "Friggin' Hell!" and prefers to insult his brother by calling him a "Friggin Meanie!", which Noah has now added to his repertoire. I was able to find this faintly amusing until Noah referred to his teacher once as a "Fricken Meanie", mispronounced but effective nonetheless. We had a little talk about swearing after that.

Regardless of Noah's misdemeanours, he still manages to have an aura of innocence about him; he is a dichotomy of boisterous recklessness and loving affection. In just about every report I have read about him, and there have been many, he is described as a "delightful" boy, one minute he will be punching you and the next playing his favourite "smooches" game, where you are smothered with sloppy wet kisses on your face. He can be like a playful puppy, which has a funny crazy-sounding Kookaburra laugh and a squeaky little speaking voice. What a character! Caleb's affection is harder to earn, but all the more precious for it. When he gives you the gift of a hug or a very rare kiss, it is heartfelt and genuine and never sloppy – a moment to be treasured.

8

Caleb's Mental Health Issues and Ear Problems.
Noah's Behavioural Tics

The stress and pressures of school took a more serious turn for Caleb last year. As he was placed in a combined year one/two class, he struggled socially with the older more mature children, but managed mostly with the academic curriculum despite finding some subjects tediously boring. He began to intensely dislike going to school and would become very resistant and anxious the night before, working his way up to full blown refusal to attend by the morning. This was difficult to manage as we wanted him to go to school as much as he was able to, but understood that he found it challenging and exhausting. It was also difficult to determine what was illness related, as he began to make himself physically sick with headaches and stomach aches, as well as his ongoing ear problems. For a period of time there, he would refuse to eat any breakfast and we would have to dress him and then literally drag him into the school grounds, where once in the classroom he would crawl under the desks to hide. The school managed this for a brief period by having the guidance counsellor talk to Caleb before class began, and he would be called to collect Caleb if he was showing signs of distress. They also tried to factor in additional break times and offer alternative playground options, but as is common, these solutions were only short term and were quickly phased out once more pressing student issues took precedent. It was suggested that Caleb might benefit from attending only part-time, but as we could never predict the days that Caleb wouldn't be able to attend he ended up having additional days at home, even when unnecessary.

We began to seriously consider the feasibility of sending both boys to the special school, as the mainstream situation was becoming untenable. We were also mindful that it is widely acknowledged that the learning gap between typical students and those with ASD usually begins to widen around the Year Three mark, when schooling expectations increase. We compromised with providing the boys with down-time or days off at our discretion, and the school was agreeable to this. Happily their ability to attend school seems to be increasing with their maturity, or maybe as I am now a working mother I just choose to ignore all minor attempts to stay home from school. By necessity I have had to adopt a more "tough love" approach. Reassuringly as both boys show academic aptitude, it is unlikely they would be required to repeat their grade levels in the immediate future, despite their frequent absences due to illness or anxiety.

At this time Caleb was also becoming more fixated on his current obsession which is cats, and was retreating further into his own private cat world, where he began to communicate via miaows, hisses, snarls and purrs, depending on his mood. It sounds funny, but it is actually quite disturbing to witness him blurring the line between his perception and reality, and is ongoing as I write this. We had adopted our beautiful cat Lola from the RSPCA when Caleb was five, and he had slowly become more attached to her, appreciating her uncomplicated affection, placidness and devotion. Caleb knows where he stands with Lola, unlike with tricky, changeable people and he began to believe he has a special communicative connection with her, thus speaking "cat talk".

As described in the book titled *All Cats Have Asperger's Syndrome*, we do think that due to Lola's need for adherence to strict routines, and her demanding behaviour, that she has "Catsberger's" and that our goldfish probably have "Fishberger's" as they like repetition too. I began to be fearful of co-morbid disorders such as schizophrenia to which we have a genetic link on Ben's side of the family as Caleb finds it easier to relate to people and the world whilst being the character of his alter-ego named Whiskas, after the cat food. This TV ad had such an impact on him that Caleb has now adopted the distinct purple of the cat tins as his favourite colour. He has developed a very elaborate make believe world of himself as "Whiskas" and me being "Mummy Cat", with "Cat Honour" points awarded for good behaviour.

This process began quite slowly and harmlessly with a rise in his love of all things cat related, then he adopted some cat mannerisms but the behaviour has now escalated to being uncontrollable. What baffled teachers, his paediatrician and a psychologist we visited, was that Caleb would also retreat into this world when he was feeling happy as well as anxious or upset, and it became apparent that this was not an attention seeking scheme for him. We had various opinions about whether to stamp out all cat related material and activities, but this approach wouldn't work anyway as he briefly moved onto howling like a werewolf when his cat world was threatened. I had even begun to play along sometimes with "Whiskas", as he was far more compliant than Caleb, and my power as "Mummy Cat" enabled me to gain Caleb's cooperation where I otherwise couldn't.

Most of Caleb's more extreme cat related meltdowns were played out at home, but his unusual behaviour was becoming more apparent to his classmates. He would either stroke them or sometimes scratch and claw near them, not often directly at them thankfully, and it became known that Caleb loved being a cat. A patient few friends would sometimes indulge in playing cats with Caleb in the playground with one of Caleb's female friends given the honorary role of "Mummy Cat". They could not satisfy Caleb's appetite for this game and they would soon move onto more age appropriate activities, once again leaving Caleb feeling despondent and different.

I will just take this opportunity, whilst on the subject of family pets, to dispel the myth that all autistic children love dogs and would benefit from having one. This is not the case as both our boys are quite fearful of unpredictable and noisy dogs, especially Noah as he was mauled by one in a park once, the dog being attracted by Noah's running, seemingly playful movements. This dog was probably only playing also, but as Noah became more terrified the dog became more aggressive and we sprinted across the park to rescue a distraught Noah, the dog having escaped his owner who was nowhere in sight.

Of course there are some dogs that the boys will tolerate, my mother's late much beloved golden retriever was one of these, and smaller calmer dogs are usually acceptable. However like all choices of family pets, this is a personal decision and I become tired of hearing "Why don't you get the boys a dog? They are really great for autistic kids". I know there are some excellent programs that match aide dogs to children with autism, and that these kids can really benefit from this interaction. These programs use the same theory underpinning giving children with autism horse riding classes, which some kids with ASD really love, but it can't be assumed that all will enjoy the same activities. So no dogs on the horizon for us, one cat and five goldfish, obviously not in the same living domiciles, are pets-a-plenty for this household.

It is not surprising therefore that Caleb's erratic behaviour coincided with a severe plummet in his self-esteem, confidence and school performance, and an escalation in his aggressive tendencies. He would go on to say worrying phrases such as "You don't love me Mummy. You hate me" during times of anxiety, unable to articulate his specific feelings. This wasn't as alarming as it may sound, because often children with autism have difficulty expressing their more complex feelings, so they tend to use extreme expressions to convey a multitude of feelings such as frustration, boredom, confusion and even unhappiness and anger. Noah tends to say that he hates us a lot, often as a reaction to simply being told "no" to a desired toy or something equally minor. He went through a stage of saying he wanted to kill us when he discovered that this had some shock value, for a brief time until I realised he didn't even have an understanding of death, as per those "cognitive gaps" already mentioned. Of course these statements aren't pleasant to receive, and we offer more appropriate alternative responses to the boys, but they are preferable to the outright physical aggression that breaks out at times.

But when Caleb began to announce that he wished he was dead, rather than go to school, and he does have a better understanding of this concept, it was time to seek professional help-stat! Caleb began receiving treatment from our current psychologist James, the aforementioned specialist in Asperger syndrome, who has provided some welcome specific strategies to deal with the cat behaviour or cat-astrophe as it has now become. Caleb is in the process of being trained to replace his "cat feelings" with human or "Caleb feelings" as we call them, James is helping him to identify what his feelings actually are, knowledge you can't take for granted with children with ASD. We are heavily rewarding him for being Caleb and not

"Whiskas" and I have also been given some firm advice not to engage in cat play with Caleb in the role of "Mummy Cat", as this reinforces his fantasy cat world and controlling tendencies. We are weathering the storm with this now, as I write, and are experiencing similar withdrawal symptoms to the "blankie" debacle. Technically, another of Caleb's comfort objects, in this case comfort world, is being dismantled.

To completely eradicate the cat obsession would be impossible and counter-productive, resulting in more anxiety for Caleb and a possible replacement with even less desirable behaviour, so we have established some guidelines. Caleb can still love cats and collect cat paraphernalia, he is still even being "Whiskas" at times but not with my participation, and has now replaced me with Noah taking on the role of "Mummy Cat". Noah doesn't usually attempt to argue with Caleb's unquestionable leadership, so happily goes along with this, until he needs rescuing from Caleb's intense dominance. We are not tackling any of these issues yet as these changes need to be approached gradually and I am busy dealing with the backlash from Caleb's anger at his perceived withdrawal of my love for him. Once again he is like that drug addict needing a fix, and is extremely volatile. Interestingly enough, Caleb reports having a physical compulsion to miaow as he says his "throat hurts because he is so used to miaowing" and he described his chest as hurting with the repressed need to be "Whiskas". Even more reasons to be sensitive in our approach to managing this complex issue.

Caleb's increasingly disturbing mental health issues coincided with his relentless aural ones, making for an exhausting time for all of us. He had been on a waiting list to receive his third set of ear grommets, and when his turn eventually came around we prepared for a straightforward day surgery procedure, after all we had been through this several times before with both boys. We didn't count on the difficulties faced with Caleb now being older and more aware of the procedures, and despite our preparation and communication with the hospital prior to the surgery day, we were all understandably nervous.

As it became apparent that Caleb's compliance would not be forthcoming the doctors ordered a pre-operation sedative for him, but he proved resistant to even this and would not relinquish his sense of control easily As the sedative took hold Caleb began to become fixated on the gadgets around him and wanted a detailed lesson on how the bed remote control worked, unfortunately his motor skills were becoming impaired and he struggled with precise movements as he made the bed go up and down repetitively. Ben and I were disconcerted by his state as he appeared to be drunk and incoherent, but he was still in our care for some time yet. Then he became angry with us as he fought his altered state of consciousness and the disorientation he was experiencing. We were familiar with this from his previous dental surgery less than a year before, but his reactions were even more extreme this time. I knew he also would fight the anaesthetic mask placed on his face in the operating theatre as he hates the smell of the "sleeping gas" as he calls it. We combated this with applying sweet smelling vanilla essence, his favourite fragrance, around the mask's edge, but he still needed to be restrained while going under.

It has always been my job to go into the operating theatres with the boys, as only one parent can, and I don't usually get very tearful anymore as I am more accustomed to it, but this time I acutely felt Caleb's confusion and pain as he thrashed about during the countdown to unconsciousness. The anaesthetist remarked on

Caleb's resistance to the medication administered, and his tenacity in clinging onto control once again. So as the procedure was not going to be long, Ben and I went off for a quick much-needed coffee (where was that rubbing alcohol again?) and consequently missed the message on my mobile as we were in a lift, advising us to hurriedly return to the recovery theatre as the procedure was finished.

We didn't need directions because as we approached the doors to the theatre we could hear Caleb's blood curdling screams; it was action stations as several nurses and a doctor tried to restrain Caleb while he thrashed around uncontrollably. They mistakenly thought he would calm down once we could make him aware of our presence, but he didn't. Instead we helped by wrapping him in a sheet and putting the bed sides up, as we knew what was to come. He cannot cope with the residual anaesthetic after surgeries and screams that he "hates feeling different" and that he can still smell and taste the gas. He becomes extremely violent and on this occasion he kicked me hard in the nose, as we stood by in shock. The nurses and the doctors hadn't experienced quite such a dramatic case as this, and weren't very equipped to handle it. Ben and I went into action mode as Caleb proceeded to vomit, tear off his sheets and try to leap out of the bed naked, with his IV line still attached. This went on for an excruciating hour, before he had periods of calmer behaviour.

We had witnessed this before too, after the dental surgery, but in that hospital he was put into a private room, cleared of furniture, to recover wrapped in sheets on the floor and out of harm's way. It was still traumatic but there was less danger of injury for Caleb or us. Once again we returned home from hospital like shell shocked war victims. You can imagine our distress when after several return clinic visits, and a lot of pain for Caleb, we discovered he had developed a blood clot in his ear, and the grommets would have to be repositioned under another general anaesthetic. This time we were fortunate enough to be placed in the private section of the hospital, due to the full public surgery lists, and I researched Caleb's condition to discover it is called Emergence Delirium.

It is common for people with neurological disorders to experience extreme reactions to anaesthetic upon regaining consciousness. We were also fortunate to have a wonderful anaesthetist who had done research into the effects of this condition on children with ASD, and consequently mixed a sedative with the anaesthetic for after the procedure, as well as before. She also took the time to write a letter for us recording this formula for any future procedures – God help us all! These are the people that truly make a difference to the quality of our lives, and for whom I have so much admiration. The ears saga continues, with trauma sustained to Caleb's ear canals, mystifying the ENTs as to precisely why he constantly experiences so much pain with them. This is not helped by his heightened sensory perceptions and low pain threshold. We are hoping that as he grows, he will outgrow these problems.

Noah's stress also began to manifest in more obvious ways throughout his first school year, with his various motor tics and repetitive movements becoming more noticeable. At times he has a constant throat clearing tic that makes him grunt compulsively. He does this virtually continuously for days, sometimes weeks, until he has a sore, hoarse throat and is distressed with being unable to stop. Before he was even diagnosed with ASD, I noticed Noah repetitively wiping his hand across his nose, despite his nose being dry, and this was one of the concerns I brought to his diagnosing psychologist, along with his toe walking and hand flapping, other stereotypical traits of autism. He sometimes repetitively blinks and then moved onto manically scratching his head, causing me to frequently check for head lice which there is never any evidence of and to cut his hair very short as he reports that his hair "bothers him". This last tic caused some social awkwardness as I felt it is necessary to reassure other parents in close proximity that Noah does not have nits but he does have autism.

It is not uncommon for Tourette syndrome to be co-morbid with ASD, and although Noah doesn't have this condition, he does have similar symptoms that we manage accordingly. Caleb's nervous habits include biting his nails down to their quick and picking his cuticles until they bleed, so that he often has to ask for bandaids at school and sometimes wears gloves due to the pain. These compulsive rituals may be lessened by Noah's previous anti-psychotic medication, although ironically one unpleasant side-effect of this med can be an increase in motor tics, making for some tricky efficacy experiments. It was also quite scary when Noah was initially adjusting to his very small dose and he fell asleep on the couch; we couldn't wake him up so the trusty paramedics were called out again, and they managed to rouse him eventually. He did gradually adjust to this sedative effect, but appeared a bit "zombie-like" at times.

During times of stress Noah will sometimes hit his head with his hand repeatedly or bang his head against a wall. Usually we can quickly redirect this behaviour and try to eliminate the cause of it, but it wasn't as easy before we knew about autism, when he would rock his cot from side to side, banging his head against the wall in order to go off to sleep. I know that I am often so tired that I could sleep through an earthquake, but that was ridiculous. Another of his delightful quirks is that he will lick your arm or face if the urge strikes him, and sometimes unknowingly if you are wearing long sleeves. He thinks this is hilarious, as does one of his previous classmates who has Global Developmental Delay and once licked the turned back of their teacher, who didn't realise that she was walking around with slobber on her clothes.

Once I took Noah out shopping to a new Target store where he became fixated by the bright fluorescent lighting reflected in the shiny mirror-like white floor. As I turned around, there to my absolute horror was Noah down on all fours licking the floor. You know, I don't think a single soul saw him do it, or else they were surprisingly tactful and quickly turned away. Maybe I should give the general public a lot more credit for their sensitivity. He has now progressed onto mirrors but I don't really worry too much, as one poor family I know of has a little boy with ASD who licks the rubbish bins in public places. That's the encouraging thing about autism, it can always be worse.

9

Social Restrictions, Respite and Domestic Tasks

Sometimes we feel like prisoners in our own home, due to the often insurmountable obstacles preventing us from venturing out. It can be impossible to find an activity that suits the boys' narrow interests, and then when we do agree on going out, we need to overcome the motion sickness experienced by the boys in the car, in order to get there. During the last couple of years, they have both started experiencing travel sickness, even on short trips, and we have tried all the usual remedies including buying them the wrist bands called sea bands that I wore in an effort to control my pregnancy morning sickness. Nothing really seems effective and Noah in particular becomes very distressed at even the prospect of a car trip, greatly further limiting our social interaction. Before accepting any invitation we weigh up the location, interest level for the boys, crowd size, time and duration of the activity and facilities there, much as if you were plotting a military invasion, and often with the same diabolical consequences. To say this takes the spontaneity out of our leisure time would be an understatement.

A friend of mine once described her two autistic boys as "taking the fun out of fun", and it certainly seems that way sometimes. Some of our friends experience similar problems but we do have others with typically developing children that are still inclined to offer breezy, casual last minute invitations or worse still change the plans or arrive *late* – a heinous crime in a time conscious household. Before facing any social gathering where we will be less likely to be able to fly under the radar and are at risk of becoming the entertainment, I take a deep breath and mentally tell myself, "Right, everyone pretend to be normal", before throwing ourselves into the lion's den. When we hired the DVD called *Little Miss Sunshine*, featuring the fabulous Toni Colette, the video shop gave us a couple of promotional badges with this phrase printed on them. I now have them pinned up on my crowded noticeboard as a permanent lifestyle mantra. The boys wanted to wear them at one point on their caps, but as I thought the irony would be lost on most people, I repossessed them.

The boys do get invited to kids' birthday parties here and there, although these invitations have dwindled in recent years. These are usually one of our more successful outings as the boys are quite used to a birthday party routine, especially if it is at our local McDonald's, and they tend to blend in with all the other screaming, sugar-hyped kids. It is the more confined, civilised social settings that really test their social skills. There is nothing like an unfamiliar crowded restaurant, or a big extended family gathering, to send us into a conniption. It seems that parenting styles are mostly falling into two warring factions in these modern times, those of the all -seeing, omnipresent, hovering "helicopter" camp and those favouring the more laissez-faire style of "free range" parenting. I think we have begun a new movement called the "24 hour CCTV surveillance" method of parenting. We simply don't have the luxury of being the relaxed and laid back, chilled out dudes we aspire to. The child rearing experts claim that any excessive parenting styles, whatever they are, are detrimental to a child's well-being, so we are in some real trouble now, just in case we weren't already aware of this.

We have attracted criticism at times for not broadening the boys socially outside of their comfort zones, but have also wisely learnt that it is more beneficial for all of us to have social success in small steps at a time. We are quite skilled now at setting boundaries in this area, sometimes to the chagrin of our families, as we are acutely aware of our limitations. Sometimes we feel that everyone else is of the opinion that they could do a better job of bringing up our kids, because ironically, we have prepared so well that it can actually appear quite easy at times.

By necessity, we have perfected the art of speed shopping, where you grab the first item of clothing, food or anything else you see in the shop, and then go home and make do with it, even if you needed something completely different. Our friends and family are quite used to receiving weird, useless gifts and Ben and I haven't exchanged a surprise present in years. I call this the "Snatch and Grab" method, and it can handily be applied to haircuts, doctor's visits and even intimate marital relations, if you are not too fussy about the quality of the result. I can proudly say that I have developed a Zen-like ability to block out the dual hammering on our *locked* bedroom door during the "conferences" that Ben and I regularly (not regularly enough for him) attend in there. I suspect the school photographers have also employed the "Snatch and Grab" method to take the boys' photos, as we are always guaranteed a laugh when we open those envelopes and find Caleb looking like Mr Bean and Noah looking like his used-car salesman sidekick. Oh well, we'll take what we can get.

One older woman whom I used to work with before the boys arrival, has "adopted" us as her yearly charity cause, I know this sounds distinctly ungrateful but I will explain. We weren't particularly close during my days of employment, so it was with surprise and far more gratitude back then that she began to bring presents over for Caleb's birthday and Christmas, and then for both boys when Noah was born; always unannounced and always during the busy dinner hour. This was in lieu of her having her own grandchildren to shower her largesse on at the time. She is quite a statuesque, forthright woman, slightly physically intimidating and prone to firing black and white style questions at me at a rapid rate. As the boys' autism became apparent, over the years they would greet these visits by excitedly snatching the presents from her hands, tearing them open immediately and flinging them away as she couldn't possibly keep up with their current obsessions, despite her attempts to wrestle the presents back and appropriately place them under the Christmas tree. She would have been more welcome had she been bearing Christmas *spirits*, rather than her unique sergeant-major style of Christmas spirit.

The boys would conveniently forget who she was in between surprise inspections, and decide to question me closely on her identity while she was standing in our lounge-room. I was usually wearing my finest trackies, not a lick of makeup and if I was really lucky the house might even have the lingering smell of Noah's recently exited evening poo. No doubt my glamorous life was then reported back to my former work colleagues in hushed sympathetic tones in the tearoom the following day. She would never actually sit down or accept an offered drink, allowing me to put the crazy scenes she was witnessing in any sort of context. So I began to feel quite resentful and in my next carefully worded thankyou card, I suggested that maybe next time she could call or email me with her planned arrival date, so I could prepare the boys, (and brace myself) for her visit. I also explained that she needn't bring presents as the boys don't really have any other close contact with her warranting them, but that she could spend some time with us if she wished. We have had a few more chaotic unscheduled visits where some strong hints were dropped on my part that perhaps she should take her bloody presents and shove them under the K-Mart wishing tree where they might be more appreciated, or better still make a donation to Autism SA. I can only assume that she knows the situation is awkward for us, as the boys are not particularly affectionate or welcoming of even their own grandparents, and that this woman insists on visiting for her own selfish reasons.

You are probably now thinking it is little wonder we don't have a huge circle of close friends, but it is difficult maintaining friendships under restricting, stressful conditions. The ones I do have, I have had for years and they are understanding of our limitations. I am also mindful of investing special time and effort when I can as we go through periods of necessary isolation. Thankfully I work with some lovely supportive colleagues and am fortunate enough to get some welcome female companionship whilst working. It is harder for our partners, as they are divided between work and stressful domestic arrangements and are often not as skilled at maintaining friendships, sometimes requiring a prod to socialise with other families. Frequently we get thrown together by circumstances with other families living with autism, but often the Dads (and in one case a Mum I know) have ASD also, making for some interesting social interactions. Just like in any group of people, not all parents of children with ASD will get along, as we all have differing ideals and goals, and sometimes fundamental clashes of methodology making friendship impossible.

I am often in the uncomfortable position of recognising

other children's ASD, sometimes before their parents do. As I
get approached for information by concerned parents about the
possibility of their child having ASD, I need to gauge how much of
my opinion they are seeking, and be careful not to provide potential
misinformation. But at the end of a day, I am just another parent and
point out that I am not a professional in the field, but can usually
refer them to someone who is. Invariably when talking to these
other parents, the subject of autism is discussed in detail. It is an
interesting phenomenon that parents of newly diagnosed autistic
children can often become so engrossed in the topic of autism that
they appear to have autism themselves. A confusing conundrum.

It is natural for us all to fall into the "autism abyss" following
a diagnosis, but it requires determination to dig ourselves out
by becoming reacquainted with former interests and pastimes.
Obviously I may not have achieved this as much as I would like,
with autism clearly being a passionate subject for me. But I do
keep a closer eye now on whether people's eyes begin to glaze
over with boredom and they start downing drinks at a rapid rate in
order to deal with the monotony; then again that is how we usually
feel on a daily basis. Some people *would* benefit from listening
to my evangelical autism rants, as there is still some breathtaking
insensitivity surrounding ASD, usually due to blissful ignorance
of the condition. I remember first hearing the term Asperger's
Syndrome being ridiculed on Rove McManus' TV show as "Arse
Burger's Syndrome". This struck a chord back then, before I even
had children of my own, and although I had no idea about the
disability at the time, I remember thinking that term would be very
hurtful for anyone dealing with the condition. Even now, someone
in our very close circle still refers to Caleb as having "Hamburger's
Disease"; I have resisted punching him in the face, but am not sure
how much longer I can hold out on this.

Another trap to be wary of falling into is the comparison game, comparing your child(ren) with ASD to another child. While it can be helpful and empowering to discover similarities with other children and parents living with ASD, it can sometimes become a competitive minefield. Even the best of friendships can become tested when vying for the same limited services and resources for our children and the severity of autism is not an easily examined, or conclusive, subject. I am sorry to say that there is usually a clear-cut pecking order of disability within any organisation we frequent, including the boys' schools. We have become more thick skinned when dealing with professionals who can only understand our boys' differences by comparing them with every other child they have encountered with ASD, and are better at deflecting these comments. The worst offenders are usually those that have limited experience with ASD, but surprisingly those that you expect to have more understanding, often don't.

After much public debate about its location and community dissension, an Autism SA southern respite house was opened recently to the relief of many local families. This respite has become a lifeline for us and many others we know living with autism, as it allows our children to stay for day visits and some overnight ones, giving us some much needed down time. It's a beautiful new secure home with great outdoor facilities, even an amazing sensory room, catering for children with autism. Our boys love going there, and this is primarily due to the competent, caring staff who are dedicated to providing the kids in their care with great experiences, often taking them to places that we find difficult to access. We are also fortunate to have discovered a wonderful carer through the Commonwealth Respite service who happens to have a son with ASD, as many carers in this field do. Not only do we know the boys are well supervised, enabling us some carefree time away, we don't feel any of the guilt or concern that we might have relying on family or friends to take on this role.

We have invested a great deal of time and renovation hours into making our home comfortable, as we spend so much time here. I have discovered some peace and joy in gardening, the ability to get away from the boys' indoor activities being its main attraction. Ben too has developed a keen interest in turning our previous dustbowl of a back lawn into a lush green carpet and can be seen out there frequently spreading fertiliser by hand and watering his oasis. He has added to his little backyard kingdom with a new garden shed and rainwater tank and we recently repainted the whole house interior as the walls had endured seven years of child abuse. Slowly we are carving out more time and inspiration to achieve the domestic goals we could only previously dream about.

As you can appreciate, holidays away from home are not a frequent event for us. We did manage to get away to the Riverland a while ago, undertaking a massive three hour drive; well it was massive for us anyway, given the car sickness situation. We had an enjoyable time, but it was not without its drama, of course. No holiday would be complete without a trip to the local country hospital in the next town, as we hastily abandoned our dinner after a screaming Noah fractured his big toe in the hotel children's play room. He had exuberantly kicked a piece of play furniture, mistaking it for having a softer texture than it did. And as "Crocs" are his usual footwear of choice, Noah's toe came off second best. Not to worry, we were so infused with family confidence upon our return that we have now booked our next adventure: a short stay in Queensland visiting the theme parks, later this year.

The only other plane trip with the boys was when I was pregnant with Noah and we went to stay with friends in Melbourne. Caleb got his first serious ear infection and vomited all over their new white leather couch. Yes it was after eating tinned spaghetti again, but thankfully the childless, career-minded couple were out hard at work so Ben and I did a super professional, frenzied cleaning operation and they were none the wiser. That time we got to visit a nice Melbourne GP before we attempted to fly baby Caleb home. All part of the joy of family holidays.

At home we have five TVs and while it's not a large house we just don't like to see each other very much, and have to fight the usual battle to keep up with Caleb's technological demands. Ben is far more skilled in this area and I am grateful for the time he spends playing games with the boys while I can get on with the far more important tasks of painting my nails and online shopping. We are not immune from our stress-relieving little obsessions either, as I go through stages of buying things such as handbags (ok, and shoes, and jewellery, and clothes, etc); but fortunately I also love patronising op shops so it's not as lethally expensive as it could be. Anyway, I have to assert some femininity living in *this* house. However, once again it is easy to start looking like we might be on the spectrum too, as our efforts to deal with the boys' compulsions become obsessions of our own. Ben is strangely obsessed with finding a quiet spot in the house, and commandeering one of the many TVs to watch cricket with a cold beer in his hand. Weird huh? The boys will ask Ben to play a game outside with them, which Ben will cheerfully do, and then before he knows it they expect him to repeat this ritual at exactly the same time every day. If I look out the window in the evening to see them all running around the yard, shooting Nerf guns at each other I know it must be 7.08p.m., signalling it's time for me to take myself off for a long, luxurious bubble bath.

10

Meltdowns

Meltdowns come in all shapes and sizes, anywhere from a brief "mini tanty" right up to a full-blown "train wreck meltdown" interchangeable with the "mother of all meltdowns", often resulting in a "mental crackdown" on our part. This is when we go completely "off our chops". We have had to develop our own language to describe these incidences, as I don't believe the necessary terminology is covered in any standard dictionary. Often a simple "@#$%*" will suffice. Noah has been stuck on a variation of the same meltdown theme for years now. His obsessions have always been toy related, reaching the extent that we can no longer allow him to get hold of a toy catalogue, so the junk mail is sifted through in the dead of the night under torchlight. Sometimes as a special treat I bring out my previously stashed hoard after the boys are in bed, and with a twinkle in my eye, present the illicit material to Ben to enjoy at his leisure. You would be amazed by how many retailers sell toys, even the crappy cheap shop catalogues have toys, and in desperate times Noah will peruse the pet toys with intent to buy. Of course he has also discovered the delights of eBay, so there is little escape, but he hasn't quite grasped the concept of patiently awaiting the purchased toy's arrival in the post. Ditto for those damn skill tester machines that he treats as his personal soft toy mart and woe betide Ben on a day when he can't win him his chosen one, due to a dodgy grabber arm.

Certain shops are now banned, the aforementioned shiny new Target being the scene of many mighty meltdowns. In one memorable visit, after Noah was refused an expensive toy, he broke free from my grip and ran headlong across the busy car park back into the shop, only for me have to drag him out all over again. I can no longer easily manhandle him now in these situations, so often resort to leaving him screaming in the aisles, pretending I don't know who he is. More like *wishing* I don't know who he is. Another facet of this obsession for Noah is his absolute loathing of any surprises: he strongly dislikes not knowing what presents he will receive, with birthdays and Christmas becoming a nightmare for months leading up to these dates. This is also extended to his need to know what is bought for everyone else, and I have now learnt not to wrap any present whatsoever without first showing him what its contents are. It doesn't matter who the recipient of the present is, even my friends or acquaintances, Noah must know or else will meltdown until it has to unwrapped and then rewrapped.

We try to alleviate this anxiety for him by using calendars and visual schedules outlining exactly when events will occur, but often have to resort to just giving him his presents early, only to have to continuously buy more up until the special day. If Noah is going to a friend's party, it is imperative that we consult him and buy exactly what present he has intended for that friend, and he will painstakingly write our their card, often tantrumming if he makes a "mistake" on it. Both Caleb and Noah have a strong need to be able to predict what will occur each day, therefore a daily schedule and preparation before any unusual event is vital.

Caleb is so sensitive to changes in routine that he used to insist on my having a pre-prepared "smoothie" in the fridge, every day after kindergarten and school for around two years. He would walk in the door and immediately grab his smoothie from the fridge and not speak until he had finished it. I figured out that his blood sugar levels must be so depleted after a busy day that he needed the instant energy from the mashed banana and yoghurt in it, as he would usually calm down after drinking it. On the occasional day that I happened to forget to have this ready, I would be greeted by an immediate meltdown and he would go "off his chops". On one memorable occasion, by the time I presented him with his smoothie he was so incandescent with rage that he threw it across the room. A large cup of sticky, milky bright pink slop dripped down the wall onto the carpet, where it proceeded to rot and stink, despite desperate, frantic carpet cleaning attempts. This eventually prompted us to rip up the carpet and to sand back the floors, and funnily enough we now don't have any carpet in the entire house.

Even though I had assured him that I could make the smoothie right away, as I hold the world record for this, taking about thirty seconds to produce an absolutely "no lumps or bumps" – always strawberry flavoured beverage. It was too late, the damage was done and I had reneged on what Caleb perceived as being a lifelong promise to always have his drink ready for him. To my great surprise one day, he informed me after he had drank his drink, that he no longer required my smoothie-making services and wouldn't be having one after school anymore. The little bugger had decided that he didn't want to eat bananas or yoghurt and was to begin to restrict his diet by eliminating the only healthy sources of nutrition he would tolerate, therefore that was the last smoothie he ever had. I actually wish that we could reinstate this stressful routine, but he now has discovered he would much rather wrangle a McDonald's frozen coke out of us at any opportunity.

During Autism 101 you get warned about "on my terms behaviour", that is the absolute lack of compromise or ability to see anyone else's point of view for many people with autism. A lack of empathy and what is called "theory of mind" also stems from these deficits. This is the ability that most of us take for granted of being able to put ourselves in "someone else's shoes" in order to see things from their angle. We also don't have the usual systems of reward at our disposal in order to reach a compromise, as the boys don't have any sense of delayed gratification due to their impatient natures. Reward charts usually cause Noah a great deal of anxiety, as he becomes stressed that the goal is unachievable and the reward therefore unattainable, so they end up causing us more problems than by not using them in the first place. That is why the nappy reward chart was miraculous. We can a have a bit more success with these for Caleb, but he soon becomes extremely pedantic and controlling, making up additional unnecessary elaborate rules, confusing us all.

We continue to work on increasing the boys' overall resilience, as this seems to be a key factor in reducing meltdowns, but it is not easy when we can't control external factors such as the weather or their personal discomfort due to heightened sensory issues. Noah will tantrum if I insist on him wearing long sleeves on a cold day, or vice versa, as his own temperature gauge is very different from the rest of ours, so I try to no longer worry about issues that don't jeopardise their health or safety, where possible. Both boys have strong aversions to certain types of shoes and clothing, making for some interesting clothing choices. The constant bickering, fighting and physical punch-ups get dealt with by "time outs" or the withdrawal of privileges if appropriate, but this is hard when out in public. It can get quite embarrassing when chasing them both around a waiting room as they run in different directions, laughing hysterically. In these situations I end up feeling so ineffectual and ridiculous, especially as the boys are getting older and now just appear to be "spoilt little brats", without a handy "I have autism" sign sitting on top of their heads.

Caleb is notorious for having a mega meltdown at the slightest provocation without any warning at all. He can go from nought to one hundred in the blink of an eye, throwing us all into the eye of the storm. He once got given a sheet of stickers from his teacher as an end of year parting gift, that he brought home with the usual array of old exercise books and multiple pages of crap (I mean precious artwork) that were destined for the recycling bin. So as I had two school bags full of work to sort through, I thought I had done very well in recognising that these stickers would need to be kept and efficiently folded the large sheet in half and filed them with Caleb's other million sticker sheets. Sorted, I thought.

Well later he moseys on into his room looking for diversion and I hear this high pitched shriek from in there. Thinking nothing of it I continue to do the dishes at the sink, with my back turned to the doorway. My first big mistake – no actually I had already made that but didn't realise what it was just yet. Caleb comes hurling out of his room and in a blur of anger pushed me forward straight into the sink. I turned around and began to say "What the ...!" when he started screaming at me that I had *folded* his sticker sheet. Meanwhile he was pummelling me as hard as his little fists could, with tears and snot running down his furious face. It took me a few seconds to realise what crime I had committed, and then I thought I could just talk him out of his anger: "No worries, the sticker sheet will be fine, it can just be unfolded" – what's the big deal hey? Next big mistake.

I should have known that he was too far gone in his tantrum to attempt to reason with. You have to realise that you are not dealing with a rational human being here; this is an Aspie in full meltdown flight. And getting to be a very tall, strong one at that, now reaching up to my shoulders. Oh yeah, I probably haven't mentioned that Ben is over six feet tall, and our sons are giants compared to most other kids their age. I usually try to comfort Caleb when he is this much out of control, as he can injure himself and ends up very frightened; any reasoning can be done later when he is able to listen, but this time the damage was already done and the sticker sheet could not be unfolded. The screaming and pummelling continued until I started to bite back a little myself, not literally but I *was* tempted. I just don't always have the time (or patience) for these dramas and when Caleb realised that my empathy wasn't forthcoming anymore, he fled off to retreat in Whiskas' world, curled up in a hidey hole in his room with his soft, polar fleece blanket over his head.

Of course I was very concerned and once again tried to comfort him, but it took a while before he would let me. Then he started sobbing that the stickers were so special and that he likes everything to stay "new looking" all the time – we are aware that the world can be a very disappointing place for Caleb, with his perfectionism not making allowances for any imperfections. Even worse was the accusation that I had folded the stickers because I "didn't love him" and wanted to hurt his feelings. This ended in a fierce "and I hate you!" from him. Well I wasn't feeling particularly endearing towards him either, but later that night we did manage a quiet moment where we reflected on the whole sorry incident – or "sticker gate" as it is now known. Caleb's teacher had the foresight to introduce a "Catastrophe Scale" that year at school, where the students could rate perceived misdemeanours from their peers by using this scale. She explained that a verbal taunt in the playground might be a one or two on the scale, but "having your arm chopped off" might be an eight, and a "plane crashing into your house" probably a ten. Some days I would welcome the plane crash scenario, but anyway the graphic detail made an impact on the kids, and we adopted this system at home too. Caleb had rated the folding of the sticker sheet as an eight, but I suggested it perhaps was probably only a one, so we compromised on a four as a meltdown repeat looked imminent.

This really highlighted for me that what we perceive as very minor incidences in our day can be incredibly important to people with ASD. I can only imagine what it would be like to live with those levels of sensitivity and I often describe to people that it is like Caleb walks around without a skin on his body. As a result of these little domestic skirmishes we are probably not the quietest of residents in our street. OK, the explosive levels of noise that we generate have caused our neighbours to shuffle past us in the street, no longer meeting our eyes. We prefer to attribute this to the probable hydroponic horticulture that we think they are indulging in and not the fact that our family could easily be featured on *A Current Affair* one night, as a prime example of living in Battlerville.

11

Lack of Personal Space and Sleeping Arrangements

Personal space is a much valued commodity around these parts. Ben and I are literally treated like a piece of furniture by the boys, a much loved, smelly old favourite couch, most of the time. They will think nothing of sitting on top of us if we have dared to sit "on their couches", and seem to love to do this more in the scorching summer months. If Ben tries to do his prescribed back exercises for his Sciatica, lying prone on the floor, he becomes an easy target to be jumped on. The boys do not have any sense of timing or ability to judge when we are more amenable to playful wrestling and we can be ambushed anywhere and anytime.

We have nicknamed Ben "The Bus", as their favourite game is to "ride" around the lounge room on top of his crawling frame. Noah looks more like a regal Sultan riding a royal elephant when he does it, but I think being called a "bus" is probably insulting enough for Ben, without pointing out any similarities to this giant creature. Caleb prefers the more kamikaze style of lassoing Ben around the neck and giving him a motivational "whip" on his backside to get him moving, and this game usually quickly degenerates into a wedgie-giving competition, as bums become handily exposed. Cushions fly and I fear for the few remaining ornaments or "specials" as the boys call them, that we have left.

People have become possessions and the giving of affection a competitive pastime for the boys. They will physically fight each other, in an attempt to bestow their affection on us, defeating the purpose as you cop a punch in the face, or Ben's favourite – a swift kick in his groin. This is another example of their "on my terms" behaviour, and while it is lovely that they can give and receive affection, it is often inappropriate and demanding. If they are feeling particularly anxious, the boys will demand a hug, every time we cross paths, and they can get very forceful making having a hug the last thing we feel like. Noah likes to creep up behind me and launch himself at my back, wrapping his arms and legs around my neck and waist, becoming a monkey on my back, like a "big sloth" as Caleb aptly describes him. If we try to have a sleep in, or even just a cup of tea in bed in the morning, the boys will competitively pile in, and wrestle to position themselves next to us; sometimes I have them sleeping on me, and the cat Lola jostling for room too, as she likes spending the night on our bed too. A long time ago we upgraded to a king size bed, but it just doesn't seem big enough now.

Sleeping has never really been a solitary pastime with both boys having a long history of playing nocturnal "musical beds". As previously described, Noah has never been a gold star sleeper, and he was diagnosed with central sleep apnoea, after an overnight sleep study when he was around three. Despite having his tonsils and adenoids removed, he still snores loudly and then will abruptly stop breathing for a few seconds, only to "reset" himself with a horrendously loud snort. Caleb bizarrely sleeps with his eyes only half closed, and when his nightlight catches his eyes, he looks like a creepy crocodile – very disconcerting when checking on him through the night.

After Noah was diagnosed with the sleep apnoea, I once again sought some professional advice regarding improving his sleeping patterns, now aware he has ASD. He was still waking frequently through the night, sometimes hourly, and we were seriously sleep deprived by then. He had also gotten into a pattern of only falling asleep in our bed with us, and unless we had the energy to transfer him to his bed and risk him waking to begin the whole process again, that's where he stayed. The person I spoke to on the Autism SA helpline (yes there is another helpline, thankfully) suggested that we could try controlled crying with Noah again; but as he was now older it could be very difficult and distressing for us all without any guarantees of success due to his neurological make-up. She gave me some useful guidelines and encouragement, and as I didn't really see any choice but to try, I steeled myself to begin that night.

It was terrible. The first night he cried for about four solid hours, and I would go in to check on him frequently, but withdraw without talking to him or giving him attention, only to have him repeatedly come out of his room, and me to wrestle him back in again. Ben was sleeping out in the rumpus room, as he needed to work the next day, and while I would have welcomed some support, I wanted to remain single-minded in my determination to succeed with this. Caleb luckily was a heavy sleeper and was oblivious to the dramas. That night passed in a blur, and with exhausted trepidation I faced the next night, where this time Noah screamed for about three hours solidly, adding head-banging the adjoining wall to his protesting repertoire. I too was in tears and called Ben in for back- up, as we both sat huddled in our bed listening to our youngest son rage all night. After another two nights of this, I conceded defeat in the worst possible way imaginable; I brought Noah into our bed again as he was beyond comforting. I have since learnt that these not so silent bedtime battles of wills are so common with children with autism that they are part of the diagnostic process.

One professional explained to me that it is "not the children with the sleep disorders, but the parents". We went on to have stages of Noah sleeping in his own bed, until he began to have night terrors and I could never bring myself to give him the sleeping tablets that he was prescribed to help us through this stage. Instead he slept in our bed again until he was confident enough to go back to his, and now we will still have either Caleb or Noah in our bed, if they are sick or unsettled, but try to avoid it if at all possible as one night is all it takes for them to establish a preferred routine. We now play soft classical music for Noah through his radio each night as he finds this soothing, Caleb would love loud rock music if we allowed it as too much peace and quiet stresses him out. Noah frequently sleepwalks, and once we woke in the middle of the night to find him standing as still as a statue at the end of our bed, staring at us with wide open eyes. Now we get a bit more restful slumber, but are woken early at the crack of dawn, usually with a toy thrust in our face and an imperative question such as "where's my Lego?" Where's *my* bloody cup of tea? – more to the point.

12

"King Mentality" and Conclusion

We came across a brilliant DVD in the local library called *Imagine Having Asperger's Syndrome*, a lecture by Melbourne clinical psychologist Dr Richard Eisenmajer who specialises in treating people with ASD. He described many people with Asperger syndrome as having a "King Mentality", that is the perception of themselves as kings and the rest of us as the serfs. He said the key to managing children with ASD is to bring them back down to the level of us serfs, thus making for more equal relations. This is certainly a challenge in our household, and one that we try to improve as the boys become enthroned on their couches shouting out insistent demands.

Some of the less likeable traits of autism can be extreme impatience and irritability, and we are on the receiving end of these on a daily basis, contributing the monotonous sense of "groundhog day" or eerie déjà vu that we rebel against. Our growing boys tend to graze on food all day due to their dietary restrictions, despite our strong preferences for set meals at the table – another battle lost by us, for now. They "order" their menu selections by calling out to us wherever we happen to be around the house, from the comfort of their couches, without lifting a pampered finger to help themselves. Due to Noah's severely limited food selections, he is now becoming tired of eating at this restaurant and bored with the lack of variety, hopefully enough to induce him to try something new one of these days. We have frustrating conversations that go like this:

"I'm hungry Mum!"

"OK what do you want to eat Noah?"

"I don't know! What's there to eat?"

"The same things as every other day Noah."

"*You tell me what's there Mum!*"

"Ok toast. I'll make you some toast."

"No! I don't want toast!"

"Well, you can get your own food then."

"*I can't make my own toast!*"

"But Noah, you just said you don't want toast to eat!"

Often when you do deliver their order, it is sent straight back to the kitchen as it is: too hot (Noah), too cold (Caleb), not crunchy enough (Noah – who will delightfully spit any soft rejected food onto his plate; sometimes the floor!), the biscuits might have "cracks" in them (Noah), or they are no longer hungry (Caleb and Noah). #$@%!

Then it's "Muuum, I need a drink with that ...!" And so on. You get the drift. Sometimes it's like living in the twilight zone. So for now, Long Live the Kings!

The stress does take its toll though, with our own health issues surfacing. We both have back problems, asthma and various seasonal aches and pains, not to mention the "mental crackdowns" that we frequently nurse each other through. I have been diagnosed with an inner ear and vestibular disorder called Meniere's disease. That comes with additional complications at times, and I am undergoing some neurological investigations for some further unexplained symptoms. Despite this, hopefully Ben and I will continue to beat the odds of the high divorce rate among families living with autism. I can't begin to imagine facing these challenges as a single parent family.

I will finish with a final medical drama to illustrate the transient nature of any sense of stability in our lives, and how it can all take a nosedive very rapidly. Last year we all had an unfortunate case of whooping cough (despite having up-to-date vaccinations, for those interested in the vaccination debate) and had to endure the indignity of phoning the surgery to pre-order face masks before we arrived at the medical centre, and then sitting in a waiting room full of curious staring people, while we wore them. The kids thought this was great fun and Noah kept lifting his off his face in order to talk, thinking his mouth wouldn't work if it was covered by the mask. He wasn't laughing quite so much when we underwent one of the quickest, most painfully invasive procedures I have ever experienced, and you know I have had quite a few. A long, metal nasal probe was inserted to what felt like the back of our brains, to collect a nasal swab to test for the whooping cough virus.

Now unfortunately I had received mine a couple of days before, and had come staggering home with my eyes watering and told all the guys about my traumatic experience and my awesome bravery. They were all ill too, but mistakenly thankful that this alien space probe procedure wasn't going to happen to them, Ben especially. So he was quite apprehensive when they too had to have it a couple of days later, and once again I wished I had kept my big fat gob shut about the impending pain, or "discomfort" as those sadist doctors like to call it. He survived it by blinking rapidly and having to suck it up, because the boys were next to be tested. I didn't want them to be subjected to this pain, and I argued with the doctor that it was unnecessary as we clearly had the same infection, to no avail. I will never forget the look on poor little Noah's face after he was advised to expect a "little tickle" as that probe went into his nose, his face just crumpled afterwards and he sobbingly stammered "I didn't like that medicine Mummy!" Another "worse parent ever" highlight. Well, there was no way we were going to catch Caleb after that, and I secretly cheered him on as he tried to bite the doctor's hand, who then had the foresight to forego testing Caleb. Yes, we have plenty of bitter sweet tragi-comic times in our family, and will no doubt have many more in the future.

So Ben and I will continue to nurture our little "diamonds" and look after ourselves and each other. We have grown in ways we couldn't have imagined since having children with disabilities, becoming less judgemental and more tolerant of others, appreciating the beauty in everyone's diversity.

When we get asked about what the future holds for Caleb and Noah, my initial glib thought is "How long is a piece of string?", meaning that we just don't know. Some people feel the reassuring need to convey absolute certitude of the boys' future independence and can foresee prestigious careers for them. However, we will be content with their happiness and quality of life, in whatever form this may take. We can't foresee their educational paths in the near future or predict their long term outcomes. We do know that we will continue to strive to give them every opportunity to reach their full potential, by doing the best job that we can. Until recently Noah wanted to go to university and study archaeology like Indiana Jones, but only if he could carry a whip, and one day he asked me, "Mum, what university would I go to if I wanted to become a super hero?", a difficult question to answer that. Who am I to say that he can't be a super hero when he grows up? His current career choice is to be a police officer – but only if he can carry a gun; so we will cross that bridge if we have to! Caleb's feet are more firmly planted on the ground with aspirations to be a computer game programmer, and a damn fine one he will be too.

> *Oh think twice, it's another day for*
> *You and me in paradise*
> *Oh think twice, it's just another day for you,*
> *You and me in paradise*

("Another Day in Paradise" by Phil Collins)

Glossary of Terms

ABA (Applied Behavioural Analysis): A systematic method of supporting and/or altering behaviour.

Adenoidectomy: The surgical removal of the adenoids.

ADHD (Attention Deficit Hyperactivity Disorder): A condition characterised by excessively inattentive, hyperactive and impulsive behaviour.

Amniocentesis: A medical procedure used in prenatal diagnosis of chromosomal abnormalities and fetal infections, in which a small amount of amniotic fluid, which contains fetal tissues, is sampled from the amniotic sac surrounding a developing foetus, and the fetal DNA is examined for genetic abnormalities.

APD (Auditory Processing Disorder): Also known as Central Auditory Processing Disorder (CAPD), it is an umbrella term for a variety of disorders that affect the way the brain processes auditory information.

ASD (Autism Spectrum Disorder): This currently refers to Autism, Asperger syndrome, and Pervasive Developmental Disorder Not Otherwise Specified (PDD-NOS). Autism Includes Autistic Disorder and Childhood Autism.

AS (Asperger Syndrome): Used for Asperger Disorder and Asperger Syndrome, an Autism Spectrum Disorder.

Autistic Savant: A person with autism who has an unusual gift or an outstanding skill or knowledge clearly above their general level of ability and above the population norm.

Central Sleep Apnoea: The repeated cessation of breathing during sleep because the brain temporarily stops sending signals to the muscles that control breathing.

Congenital Muscular Torticollis: A condition that occurs at birth or up to two months of age, where the child's head is tilted to one side; also sometimes called wryneck.

DECD (previously DECS): Department of Education and Children's Development.

DSM 5 (previously the DSM V): The planned fifth edition of the American Psychiatric Association's (APA) *Diagnostic and Statistical Manual of Mental Disorders.*

Echolalia: The automatic repetition of vocalisations made by another person.

Ectopic Pregnancy: An abnormal pregnancy that occurs outside the womb (uterus).

ECV (External Cephalic Version): A process by which a breech baby can sometimes be turned from buttocks or foot first to head first.

Emergence Delirium: A post-operative dissociated state of consciousness often characterised by severe agitation.

Global Developmental Delay: A delay in two or more important areas of development. These areas include motor skills, speech and language skills, academic skills, learning ability, social and emotional skills and self-help skills.

Grommets: Tiny plastic tubes which are inserted through a small cut in the eardrum to allow air into the middle ear until the Eustachian tube begins to function normally.

HFA (High Functioning Autism): An informal term used to describe autistic people who are considered to have more intellectual and cognitive abilities than others on the Autism Spectrum; this is not a formal diagnostic term.

HG (Hyperemesis Gravid arum): A severe form of morning sickness, with excessive pregnancy-related nausea and/or vomiting that prevents adequate intake of food and fluids.

Hyperlexia: A syndrome characterised by an intense fascination with letters or numbers and an advanced reading ability.

IQ (Intelligence Quotient): A score derived from one of several different standardised tests designed to assess intellectual abilities.

Meniere's disease: A disorder of the inner ear that can affect hearing and balance to a varying degree. It is characterised by episodes of vertigo, low pitched tinnitus and hearing loss.

NEP (Negotiated Education Plan): An intervention plan that is devised, usually within an educational setting, to provide services to a child who has demonstrated special learning needs.

Operant Conditioning: A method of learning that occurs through rewarding desirable behaviours, and ignoring undesirable ones.

NT (Neurotypical): Used to describe people who are not on the Autism Spectrum and who generally have typical development, linguistic and social skills.

Rotavirus: The most common cause of severe diarrhoea among infants and young children.

RSV (Respiratory Syncytial Virus): A virus that causes respiratory infections. Illness is common in children under two years of age. In this age group RSV can cause bronchiolitis (inflammation of the small breathing tubes of the lung) and pneumonia (infection of the lung).

Sleep Apnoea (or Obstructive Sleep Apnoea): When the walls of the throat come together or collapse during sleep, blocking off the upper part of the airway.

Tonsillectomy: The surgical removal of the tonsils.

TS (Tourette syndrome): A neurological disorder characterised by involuntary, irresistible body movements and vocalisations.

Ventolin (Albuterol inhalation): Used to treat bronchospasm in people with asthma symptoms.

Wechsler Intelligence Scale for Children (WISC) and the *Wechsler Preschool and Primary Scale of Intelligence* (WPPSI): Consist of a series of short sub tests that are used to assess cognitive ability.

Acknowledgements

Two years ago I woke up one day and decided to write this book. I have many people to thank for this two year journey from inspiration to publication. Firstly I thank my family – our beautiful two boys for simply being themselves and Ben for his unerring loyalty and endless encouragement during my times of doubt. My colourful artist Mum (and her flattering cover design – I have never looked so stylish!) and all the rest of our combined clans.

Big thanks to my co-contributors Robyn Young, Jon Martin and Jason Leffers, Connor Court Publishing, Autism SA, my DECD colleagues and for the enthusiasm from our wonderful friends, neighbours and autism community.

About the Author

I live with my husband Ben, our two children Caleb and Noah and our cat Lola, in Adelaide, South Australia. I completed a Bachelor of Arts majoring in English Literature after finishing school, and was selected as one of two final candidates for a cadetship with *The Advertiser* newspaper. Unfortunately I was not selected for that intake, but was advised to apply again the following year as I had a stronger chance of being successful having already undertaken the application process. As my patience didn't extend that far, I proceeded to pursue my part-time career path of working as a store manager for McDonald's. As I already had achieved my Certificate IV Diploma in Management, I went on to manage a busy metro McDonald's store, and won an academic award at one of the business conferences I attended.

My next career move was into telecommunications and then banking before embarking on my most challenging role of motherhood. During my lengthy eight year "home detention" (I mean sabbatical!) I had an article published by *Practical Parenting* in January 2004, and was interviewed for our local *Messenger* newspaper and another parenting magazine called *South Kids*. Ben and I were also nominated in 2009 for Autism SA's Parent/Carer recognition award, for our contribution to the boys' early intervention programme. In May 2011 I began work as a SSO (School Services Officer) at the school our boys attend, and work with a wide range of students with special needs. I established a support group for the parents of these children at the school, but unfortunately facilitating it was not compatible with my increasing workload. I now have the opportunity to support both the students and the parents in my current role, which I find immensely rewarding.

www.ingramcontent.com/pod-product-compliance
Lightning Source LLC
Chambersburg PA
CBHW070927270326
41927CB00011B/2754